Table of Contents

Introduction

The National Council of Teachers of English and the International Reading Association prepared standards for the English language arts. These standards "grew out of current research and theory about how students learn—in particular, how they learn language." These standards address "what students should know and be able to do in the English language arts."

One standard is that students should be able to communicate effectively by learning the "language of wider communication," the forms of the English language that are most commonly identified as standard English. Students must recognize the importance of audience when they write and speak so they will be able to use the appropriate form of language for the intended audience. The standards acknowledge that "students need guidance and practice to develop their skills in academic writing. . . . They need to understand the varying demands of different kinds of writing tasks and to recognize how to adapt tone, style, and content for the particular task at hand." Again, students must "consider the needs of their audiences as they compose, edit, and revise."

Another standard emphasizes that "students apply knowledge of language structure, language conventions. . . ." Students need practice with accepted language conventions (e.g., capitalization, punctuation, grammar) in order to develop awareness and consistent application in their writing.

Language Practice is a program designed for students who require additional practice in the basics of effective writing and speaking. Focused practice in key grammar, usage, mechanics, and composition areas helps students gain ownership of essential skills. The logical sequence of the practice exercises, combined with a clear and concise format, allows for easy and independent use.

National Council of Teachers of English and International Reading Association, *Standards for the English Language Arts*, 1996.

Organization

Language Practice provides systematic, focused attention to just one carefully selected skill at a time. Rules are clearly stated at the beginning of each lesson. Key terms are introduced in bold type. The rules are then illustrated with examples and followed by meaningful practice exercises.

Lessons are organized around a series of units. They are arranged in a logical sequence beginning with vocabulary; progressing through sentences, grammar and usage, and mechanics; and culminating with composition skills.

Grades 3 through 8 include a final unit on study skills, which can be assigned as needed. This unit includes such skills as organizing information, following directions, using a dictionary, using the library, and choosing appropriate reference sources.

Skills are reviewed thoroughly in a two-page test at the conclusion of each unit. These unit tests are presented in a standardized test format. The content of each unit is repeated and expanded in subsequent levels as highlighted in the skills correlation chart on pages 6 and 7.

Use

Throughout the program, *Language Practice* stresses the application of language principles. In addition to matching, circling, or underlining elements in a predetermined sentence, lessons ask students to use what they have learned in an original sentence or in rewriting a sentence.

Language Practice is designed for independent use by students who have had instruction in the specific skills covered in these lessons. Copies of the activities can be given to individuals, pairs of students, or small groups for completion. They can also be used as a center activity. If students are familiar with the content, the worksheets can be homework for reviewing and reinforcing skills.

From the beginning, students feel comfortable with the format of the lessons. Each lesson is introduced with a rule at the top of the page and ends with a meaningful exercise at the bottom of the page. Each lesson is clearly labeled, and directions are clear and uncomplicated. Because the format is logical and consistent and the vocabulary is carefully controlled, most students can use *Language Practice* with a high degree of independence. As the teacher, this allows you the time needed to help students on a one-to-one basis.

Special Feature

The process approach to teaching writing provides success for most students. *Language Practice* provides direct support for the teaching of composition and significantly enhances those strategies and techniques commonly associated with the process-writing approach.

Each book includes a composition unit that provides substantial work with important composition skills, such as considering audience, writing topic sentences, selecting supporting details, taking notes, writing reports, and revising and proofreading. Also included in the composition unit is practice with various prewriting activities, such as clustering and brainstorming, which play an important role in process writing. The composition lessons are presented in the same rule-plus-practice format as in other units.

Additional Notes

- Parent Communication. Sign the *Letter to Parents* and send it home with the students. This letter offers suggestions for parental involvement to increase learner success.

- Assessment Test. Use the Assessment Test on pages 8 through 11 to determine the skills your students need to practice.

- Language Terms. Provide each student with a copy of the list of language terms on page 12 to keep for reference throughout the year. Also place a copy in the classroom language arts center for reference.

- Center Activities. Use the worksheets as center activities to give students the opportunity to work cooperatively.

- Have fun. The activities use a variety of strategies to maintain student interest. Watch your students' language improve as skills are applied in structured, relevant practice!

Dear Parent,

During this school year, our class will be working with a language program that covers the basics of effective writing and speaking. To increase your child's language skills, we will be completing activity sheets that provide practice to ensure mastery of these important skills.

From time to time, I may send home activity sheets. To best help your child, please consider the following suggestions:

- Provide a quiet place to work.
- Go over the rules, examples, and directions together.
- Encourage your child to do his or her best.
- Check the lesson when it is complete.
- Go over your child's work, and note improvements as well as concerns.

Help your child maintain a positive attitude about language skills. Let your child know that each lesson provides an opportunity to have fun and to learn. If your child expresses anxiety about these skills, help him or her understand what causes the stress. Then talk about ways to deal with it in a positive way.

Above all, enjoy this time you spend with your child. He or she will feel your support, and skills will improve with each activity completed.

Thank you for your help!

Cordially,

Skills Correlation

Vocabulary	1	2	3	4	5	6	7	8
Sound Words (Onomatopoeia)	■							
Rhyming Words	■	■						
Synonyms	■	■	■	■	■	■	■	■
Antonyms	■	■	■	■	■	■	■	■
Homonyms	■	■	■	■	■	■	■	■
Multiple Meanings/Homographs	■	■	■	■	■	■	■	■
Prefixes and Suffixes			■	■	■	■	■	■
Base and Root Words			■	■	■	■	■	■
Compound Words			■	■	■	■	■	■
Contractions			■	■	■	■	■	■
Idioms						■	■	■
Connotation/Denotation						■	■	■

Sentences	1	2	3	4	5	6	7	8
Word Order in Sentences	■	■						
Recognizing a Sentence	■	■	■	■	■	■	■	■
Subjects and Predicates	■	■	■	■	■	■	■	■
Types of Sentences	■	■	■	■	■	■	■	■
Compound/Complex Sentences			■	■	■	■	■	■
Sentence Combining			■	■	■	■	■	■
Run-On Sentences			■	■	■	■	■	■
Independent and Subordinate Clauses							■	■
Compound Subjects and Predicates						■	■	■
Direct and Indirect Objects							■	■
Inverted Word Order						■	■	■

Grammar and Usage	1	2	3	4	5	6	7	8
Common and Proper Nouns	■	■	■	■	■	■	■	■
Singular and Plural Nouns	■	■	■	■	■	■	■	■
Possessive Nouns			■	■	■	■	■	■
Appositives						■	■	■
Verbs	■	■	■	■	■	■	■	■
Verb Tense	■	■	■	■	■	■	■	■
Regular/Irregular Verbs	■	■	■	■	■	■	■	■
Subject/Verb Agreement		■	■	■	■	■	■	■
Verb Phrases						■	■	■
Transitive and Intransitive Verbs							■	■
Verbals: Gerunds, Participles, and Infinitives							■	■
Active and Passive Voice							■	■
Mood								■
Pronouns	■	■	■	■	■	■	■	■
Antecedents							■	■
Articles	■	■	■					
Adjectives	■	■	■	■	■	■	■	■
Correct Word Usage (e.g. *may/can, sit/set*)	■	■	■	■	■	■	■	■
Adverbs			■	■	■	■	■	■
Prepositions						■	■	■
Prepositional Phrases						■	■	■
Conjunctions						■	■	■
Interjections						■	■	■
Double Negatives								■

Capitalization and Punctuation	1	2	3	4	5	6	7	8
Capitalization: First Word in Sentence	■	■	■	■	■	■	■	
Capitalization: Proper Nouns	■	■	■	■	■	■	■	■
Capitalization: in Letters		■	■	■	■	■	■	■

Capitalization and Punctuation (cont'd)	1	2	3	4	5	6	7	8
Capitalization: Abbreviations		■	■	■	■	■	■	■
Capitalization: Titles		■	■	■	■	■	■	■
Capitalization: Proper Adjectives					■	■	■	■
End Punctuation	■	■	■	■	■	■	■	■
Commas		■	■	■	■	■	■	■
Apostrophes in Contractions		■	■	■	■	■	■	■
Apostrophes in Possessives			■	■	■	■	■	■
Quotation Marks		■	■	■	■	■	■	■
Colons/Semicolons						■	■	■
Hyphens						■	■	■
Composition								
Expanding Sentences					■	■	■	■
Writing a Paragraph		■	■	■	■	■	■	■
Paragraphs: Topic Sentence (main idea)		■	■	■	■	■	■	■
Paragraphs: Supporting Details		■	■	■	■	■	■	■
Order In Paragraphs		■	■	■	■	■	■	
Writing Process:								
Establishing Purpose			■	■		■	■	■
Audience					■	■	■	■
Topic			■	■	■	■	■	■
Outlining				■		■	■	■
Clustering/Brainstorming					■		■	■
Notetaking						■	■	
Revising/Proofreading					■	■	■	■
Types of Writing:								
Letter	■	■	■			■		
"How-to" Paragraph				■				
Invitation				■				
Telephone Message				■				
Conversation				■				
Narrative Paragraph				■				
Comparing and Contrasting					■			
Descriptive Paragraph					■			
Report						■		
Interview							■	
Persuasive Composition								■
Readiness/Study Skills								
Grouping	■							
Letters of Alphabet	■							
Listening	■	■						
Making Comparisons	■	■						
Organizing Information	■	■	■					
Following Directions	■	■	■	■	■			
Alphabetical Order	■	■	■	■	■	■	■	■
Using a Dictionary:								
Definitions		■	■	■	■	■	■	■
Guide Words/Entry Words		■	■	■	■	■	■	■
Syllables			■	■	■	■	■	■
Multiple Meanings						■	■	■
Word Origins						■	■	■
Parts of a Book						■	■	■
Using the Library						■	■	■
Using Encyclopedias				■	■	■	■	■
Using Reference Books						■	■	■
Using the *Readers' Guide*							■	■
Choosing Appropriate Sources						■	■	■

Name _____ Date _____

Assessment Test

A. Write S before each pair of synonyms, A before each pair of antonyms, and H before each pair of homonyms.

_____ **1.** full, empty   _____ **3.** journal, notebook

_____ **2.** lead, led   _____ **4.** would, wood

B. Write the homograph for the pair of meanings.

_____ **a.** a container   **b.** to be able

C. Write P before each word with a prefix, S before each word with a suffix, and C before each compound word.

_____ **1.** joyous   _____ **3.** disappear

_____ **2.** outcome   _____ **4.** mislead

D. Write the words that make up each contraction.

_____ _____ **1.** can't   _____ _____ **2.** they'll

E. Underline the word in parentheses that has the more positive connotation.

Our (nosy, curious) neighbor peeked over the fence.

F. Circle the letter of the idiom that means <u>out of favor</u>.

a. down in the dumps   **b.** in the doghouse

G. Write D before the declarative sentence, IM before the imperative sentence, E before the exclamatory sentence, and IN before the interrogative sentence. Then circle the simple subject, and underline the simple predicate in each sentence.

_____ **1.** Who is going with us?   _____ **3.** Don't worry about a thing.

_____ **2.** I feel awful!   _____ **4.** It is best to just wait.

H. Write CS before the sentence that has a compound subject. Write CP before the sentence that has a compound predicate.

_____ **1.** The dog growled and barked.

_____ **2.** Broccoli and carrots are tasty vegetables.

I. Write CS before the compound sentence. Write RO before the run-on sentence. Write I before the sentence that is in inverted order.

_____ **1.** We had been there once before, it was familiar to me.

_____ **2.** Around the corner sped the getaway car.

_____ **3.** Time was running out, and darkness was falling.

J. Underline the common nouns, and circle the proper nouns in the sentence.

The police officer told Paul that Judge Hawkins was the person who would decide.

Name _____   Date _____

K. Write the correct possessive noun to complete the second sentence.

The car of her friend was stolen. Her _____ car was stolen.

L. Underline the appositive in the sentence. Circle the noun it identifies or explains.

Nolan Ryan, a baseball star, is signing autographs at the store.

M. Underline the verb phrase, and circle the helping verb.

He will soon discover the error in his plan.

N. Write past, present, or future to show the tense of each underlined verb.

_____ 1. Yesterday it rained very hard.

_____ 2. Soon the clouds will disappear.

_____ 3. Sunny days are my favorite.

O. Circle the correct verbs in each sentence.

1. Rosa (fly, flew) to Paris and (went, gone) to see the Eiffel Tower.

2. She (drink, drank) the soda and (throw, threw) the can in the recycling bin.

3. The ice (frozen, froze) hard but (broke, broken) up in the spring.

P. Write SP before the sentence that has a subject pronoun, OP before the sentence that has an object pronoun, PP before the sentence that has a possessive pronoun, and IP before the sentence that has an indefinite pronoun. Circle the pronoun in each sentence.

_____ 1. You should take a nap.   _____ 3. A smile was her answer.

_____ 2. Nobody knew what happened.   _____ 4. Frank didn't even hear us.

Q. On the line before each sentence, write adjective or adverb to describe the underlined word.

_____ 1. These are my favorite books.

_____ 2. He eats here regularly.

_____ 3. You are too hasty.

_____ 4. She is an actor.

R. Circle the correct word in each sentence.

1. (May, Can) you see from here?

2. You must (teach, learn) to be patient.

3. Just (sit, set) your shoes over there.

4. She (lied, laid) down the book.

5. He (doesn't, don't) want to go.

S. Underline each prepositional phrase twice. Circle each preposition. Underline the conjunctions once.

You can either wait in the car or outside the door.

T. **Rewrite the letter. Use capital letters and punctuation marks where needed.**

832 southern star

helena mt 95097

aug 27 19___

dear edward

i have the information you wanted ____ did you ever think id get it to you this quickly ____
well its time i surprised you ____ heres what you should bring six cartons of orange juice forty
five paper cups and three bags of ice ____ what a breakfast party this will be ____

your friend

bill

_____

_____

_____

_____

_____

_____

_____

_____

_____

_____

U. **Write a topic sentence and two sentences with descriptive supporting details on the topic of home safety.**

_____

_____

_____

V. **Number the steps for writing a report in order.**

_____ **1.** Write the report.   _____ **4.** Look in an encyclopedia.

_____ **2.** Organize your research questions.   _____ **5.** Write information in your own words.

_____ **3.** Revise and proofread your report.   _____ **6.** Make an outline.

W. Circle the part that does <u>not</u> belong in a business letter.

heading   closing   title   signature   body   greeting

Name _____   Date _____

X. Use the dictionary entry below to answer the questions.

> **carpet** (kär′ pit) *n.* **1.** a thick floor covering; rug: *She cleaned the carpet.*
> **2.** a surface like a rug: *A carpet of leaves covered the ground.*

1. What part of speech is the word carpet?_____

2. Would carport come before or after carpet in the dictionary?_____

3. Would cart/cast or care/carrot be the guide words for carpet? _____

4. Write the number of the definition for carpet in this sentence: The fawn lay on a carpet of grass._____

5. Write carpet separated into syllables. _____

Y. Use the catalog card below to answer the questions.

> ```
>                  GRAND CANYON (ARIZ.)
>     979.132
>     R39       Rawlins, Carol.
>                   The Grand Canyon.
>                   Austin, TX: Raintree/Steck-Vaughn, ©1995.
>                   64p.: col. illus.
> ```

1. Who is the author?_____

2. What is the book's call number? _____

3. When was the book published?_____

4. Who is the publisher?_____

5. How many pages does the book have?_____

Z. Write the source from the box that you would use to find the information listed.

> | dictionary | card catalog | encyclopedia | atlas |

_____   **1.** a map of the world

_____   **2.** an article on Africa

_____   **3.** how to divide a word

_____   **4.** to locate a book by Mark Twain

_____   **5.** the meaning of a word

_____   **6.** information about recycled materials

Language Terms

abbreviation a short form of a word

action verb tells an action that the subject is doing

adjective describes a noun by telling which one, what kind, or how many

adverb describes a verb, an adjective, or another adverb

antonym has the opposite meaning of another word

apostrophe a mark used to show where a letter or letters have been left out of a contraction

appositive a noun or phrase that identifies or explains the noun it follows

common noun names any one of a class of objects

complete predicate the part of a sentence that includes all the words that state action or condition of the subject

complete subject the part of a sentence that includes all the words that tell who or what the sentence is about

compound predicate two predicates joined by or, and, or but that have one subject

compound sentence two simple sentences joined by words such as and, but, so, and or

compound subject two subjects joined by and that have one predicate

compound word a word made up of two or more words

conjunction a word used to join words or groups of words

connotation the meaning of a word that suggests something positive or negative

contraction a word formed by joining two other words

declarative sentence a sentence that makes a statement

demonstrative adjective an adjective that points out a specific person or thing

denotation the exact meaning of a word as stated in the dictionary

exclamatory sentence a sentence that expresses strong or sudden feeling

helping verb used to help the main verb of the sentence

homograph a word that has the same spelling as another word, but a different meaning and sometimes a different pronunciation

homonym a word that sounds like another word, but has a different meaning and is spelled differently

idiom an expression that has a meaning different from the usual meanings of the individual words within it

imperative sentence a sentence that expresses a command or a request

indefinite pronoun a pronoun that does not refer to a specific person or thing

interjection a word or group of words that expresses emotion

interrogative sentence a sentence that asks a question

inverted order the order of a sentence when all or part of the predicate comes before the subject

limiting adjective the articles a, an, and the

linking verb a verb that connects the subject of a sentence with a noun or adjective that comes after the verb

natural order the order of a sentence when the subject comes before all or part of the predicate

noun a word that names a person, place, thing, or quality

object pronoun a pronoun used after an action verb or preposition

paragraph a group of sentences about one main idea

plural noun a noun that names more than one person, place, thing, or quality

possessive noun a noun that tells who or what owns the noun that follows

possessive pronoun a pronoun that tells who or what owns something

predicate the part of a sentence that tells what the subject does or what happens to the subject

prefix a syllable added to the beginning of a base word that changes the meaning of the word

preposition a word that shows the relationship of a noun or a pronoun to another word in the sentence

prepositional phrase a group of words that begins with a preposition and ends with a noun or pronoun

pronoun a word that takes the place of a noun

proper adjective an adjective that is formed from a proper noun

proper noun a noun that names a particular person, place, or thing and is capitalized

quotation tells the exact words a person said

run-on sentence two or more sentences that run together without correct punctuation

sentence a group of words that expresses a complete thought

simple predicate the verb in the predicate part of a sentence

simple sentence a sentence that has one subject and one predicate

simple subject the main word in the subject part of a sentence

singular noun names one person, place, thing or quality

subject the part of a sentence that tells who or what the sentence is about

subject pronoun a pronoun used as the subject or as part of the subject of the sentence

suffix a syllable added to the end of a base word that changes the meaning of the word

synonym a word that has the same or nearly the same meaning as one or more other words

verb a word that expresses action, being, or state of being

verb phrase a main verb and one or more other verbs

verb tense tells the time expressed by the verb

Name _____   Date _____

Synonyms and Antonyms

> ■ A **synonym** is a word that has the same or nearly the same meaning as one or more other words.   EXAMPLES: joy – happiness   choose – pick

A. Write a synonym for each word below.

1. small _____
2. swiftly _____
3. weary _____
4. pretty _____

5. large _____
6. awful _____
7. lad _____
8. forest _____

9. cry _____
10. leap _____
11. wealthy _____
12. ugly _____

B. Circle the word in parentheses that is a synonym for the underlined word in each sentence.

1. (finish, begin)   When you start to write, think about your audience.
2. (fall, spring)   The colors of autumn leaves are breathtaking.
3. (sick, well)   Last week I was ill with the flu.
4. (tried, tired)   He was exhausted after the marathon.
5. (clothes, close)   I tried to shut the door, but it was stuck.

> ■ An **antonym** is a word that has the opposite meaning of another word.
>   EXAMPLES: hot – cold   late – early

C. Write an antonym for each word below.

1. good _____
2. old _____
3. dull _____
4. thick _____

5. tall _____
6. crooked _____
7. happy _____
8. remember _____

9. ugly _____
10. near _____
11. obey _____
12. rich _____

D. Circle the word in parentheses that is an antonym for the underlined word in each sentence.

1. (heavy, hard)   The donkey strained under its light load.
2. (last, late)   The early morning sun streamed in the window.
3. (fine, kind)   Jerry gave the dog a mean pat on the head.
4. (empty, old)   I tried to pour some milk, but the carton was full.
5. (frowned, found)   Isabel lost her favorite book.

Homonyms

> ■ A **homonym** is a word that sounds the same as another word but has a different spelling and a different meaning.
> EXAMPLES: to – two – too   sum – some

A. Underline the correct homonym(s) in each sentence below.

1. The couple walked for a mile along the (beech, beach).

2. Are there any (dear, deer) in these hills?

3. How much do you (way, weigh)?

4. Who broke this window (pane, pain)?

5. I have (to, too, two) go (to, too, two) the sale with those (to, too, two) people.

6. Laurie (knew, new) how to play a (new, knew) word game.

7. Juan and Luis spent a week at (there, their) friends' ranch.

8. Those boys (ate, eight) (ate, eight) of the apples we had just bought.

9. I like to walk by the (see, sea) at dusk.

10. (Wring, Ring) the bell, Matt.

11. Did you see what she brought (hear, here)?

12. He cannot (write, right) with his (write, right) hand.

13. Who has not (read, red) the magazine?

14. He found it cheaper to (buy, by) his pencils (buy, by) the box.

15. Chris told his niece a fairy (tale, tail).

B. Write a homonym for each word below.

1. hall _____	11. flower _____	21. our _____
2. threw _____	12. stair _____	22. sea _____
3. weak _____	13. pale _____	23. right _____
4. there _____	14. ring _____	24. peace _____
5. heard _____	15. soar _____	25. no _____
6. here _____	16. sale _____	26. grate _____
7. by _____	17. won _____	27. way _____
8. pane _____	18. aisle _____	28. cent _____
9. heal _____	19. rode _____	29. dew _____
10. blew _____	20. meet _____	30. forth _____

Homographs

> ■ A **homograph** is a word that has the same spelling as another word but a different meaning and sometimes a different pronunciation.
> EXAMPLE: bow, meaning "to bend the upper part of the body forward in respect," and bow, meaning "a weapon for shooting arrows"

vault	checks	interest

A. Fill in each blank with a homograph from the box. Use each homograph twice.

1. With a bank account, you can write _____ to pay for things.

2. She looked with great _____ at the painting.

3. He used a long pole to _____ over the jump.

4. My savings account pays _____ on the money I keep in it.

5. José keeps his stamp collection locked in a _____ .

6. She wrote small _____ beside each item on the list.

B. Circle the letter of the correct definition for each underlined homograph. Then write a sentence using the other meaning of the homograph.

1. Put your coins in the bank.

   a. a place where people save money   **b.** the ground along a river

   _____

2. If you hide your bank, be sure to remember where you put it.

   a. keep out of sight   **b.** the skin of an animal

   _____

3. Some people keep their money in a safe.

   a. a metal box with a lock   **b.** free from danger

   _____

4. There are only two people who have the key to open the safe.

   a. a piece of metal to open a lock   **b.** a low island or reef

   _____

5. Many people have an account at a bank.

   a. explanation   **b.** an amount of money

   _____

Name _____ Date _____

Prefixes

- A **prefix** added to the beginning of a base word changes the meaning of the word.
  - EXAMPLE: un-, meaning "not," + the base word <u>done</u> = <u>undone</u>, meaning "not done"
- Some prefixes have one meaning, and others have more than one meaning.

  EXAMPLES:

prefix	meaning
im-, in-, non-, un-	not
dis-, in-, non-	opposite of, lack of, not
mis-	bad, badly, wrong, wrongly
pre-	before
re-	again

A. Add the prefix <u>un-</u>, <u>im-</u>, <u>non-</u>, or <u>mis-</u> to the base word in parentheses. Write the new word in the sentence. Then write the definition of the new word on the line after the sentence. Use a dictionary if necessary.

1. It is _____ (practical) to put a new monkey into a cage with other monkeys.

   _____

2. The monkeys might _____ (behave) with a newcomer among them.

   _____

3. They will also feel quite _____ (easy) for a number of days or even weeks.

   _____

4. Even if the new monkey is _____ (violent) in nature, the others may harm it.

   _____

5. Sometimes animal behavior can be quite _____ (usual).

   _____

B. Underline each prefix. Write the meaning of each word that has a prefix.

1. unexpected guest _____

2. really disappear _____

3. disagree often _____

4. misspell a name _____

5. preview a movie _____

6. reenter a room _____

7. misplace a shoe _____

8. impossible situation _____

9. nonstop reading _____

10. unimportant discussion _____

11. insane story _____

12. prejudge a person _____

Suffixes

- A **suffix** added to the end of a base word changes the meaning of the word.
  EXAMPLE: -ful, meaning "full of," + the base word <u>joy</u> = <u>joyful</u>, meaning "full of joy"
- Some suffixes have one meaning, and others have more than one meaning.

EXAMPLES:	**suffix**	**meaning**
	-able	able to be, suitable or inclined to
	-al	relating to, like
	-ful	as much as will fill, full of
	-less	without, that does not
	-ous	full of
	-y	having, full of

A. Add a suffix from the list above to the base word in parentheses. Write the new word. Then write the definition of the new word on the line after the sentence. Do not use any suffix more than once.

1. Switzerland is a _____ country. (mountain)

   _____

2. If you visit there, it is _____ to have a walking stick. (help)

   _____

3. Many tourists visit the country's _____ mountains to ski each year. (snow)

   _____

4. The Swiss people have a great deal of _____ pride. (nation)

   _____

5. Many Swiss are _____ about several languages. (knowledge)

   _____

B. Underline each suffix. Write the meaning of each word that has a suffix.

1. breakable toy _____

2. endless waves _____

3. hazardous path _____

4. inflatable raft _____

5. poisonous snake _____

6. dependable trains _____

7. humorous program _____

8. tearful goodbye _____

9. bumpy ride _____

10. careless driver _____

11. natural food _____

12. magical wand _____

Contractions

> - A **contraction** is a word formed by joining two other words.
> - An **apostrophe** shows where a letter or letters have been left out.   EXAMPLE: do not = don't
> - <u>Won't</u> is an exception.   EXAMPLE: will not = won't

A. Underline each contraction. Write the words that make up each contraction on the line.

1. Stingrays look as if they're part bird, part fish. _____

2. Stingrays cover themselves with sand so they won't be seen. _____

3. There's a chance that waders might step on a stingray and get stung. _____

4. That's a painful way to learn that you shouldn't forget about stingrays.

   _____   _____

5. Until recently, stingrays weren't seen very often. _____

6. It doesn't seem likely, but some stingrays will eat out of divers' hands. _____

7. Because its mouth is underneath, the stingray can't see what it's eating.

   _____   _____

8. Once they've been fed by hand, they'll flutter around for more.

   _____   _____

9. It's hard to believe these stingrays aren't afraid of humans.

   _____   _____

10. To pet a stingray, they'd gently touch its velvety skin. _____

B. Find the pairs of words that can be made into contractions. Underline each pair. Then write the contraction each word pair can make on the lines following the sentences.

1. I have never tried scuba diving, but I would like to.

   _____   _____

2. It is a good way to explore what is under the water.

   _____   _____

3. First, I will need to take lessons in the pool. _____

4. Then I can find out what to do if the equipment does not work. _____

Compound Words

> - A **compound word** is a word that is made up of two or more words. The meaning of a compound word is related to the meaning of each individual word.
>   EXAMPLE: sun + glasses = sunglasses, meaning "glasses to wear in the sun"
> - Compound words may be written as one word, as hyphenated words, or as two separate words.
>   EXAMPLES: highway   high-rise   high school

A. Answer the following questions.

1. Something that has sharp, curved points extending backward is said to be barbed.

   What is barbed wire? _____

2. Dry means "without water." What does dry-clean mean? _____

3. Head means "a heading." What is a headline? _____

4. A deputy is "a person appointed to take the place of another."

   What is a deputy marshal? _____

5. Bare means "without a covering." What does bareback mean? _____

6. A road is a route. What is a railroad? _____

7. A paper is a type of document. What is a newspaper? _____

8. Blue is a color. What is a blueberry? _____

B. Combine words from the box to make compound words. Use the compound words to complete the sentences. You will use one word twice.

cut	every	fore	hair	head	where
loud	news	speaker	stand	thing	

1. Bob's hair covered his _____.

2. He knew it was time to get a _____.

3. He saw a truck hit a fire hydrant, which sprayed water _____.

4. The corner _____ was soaked.

5. A police officer used a _____ to direct traffic.

6. It was so exciting, Bob forgot about _____, including his haircut!

Connotation/Denotation

> ■ The **denotation** of a word is its exact meaning as stated in a dictionary.
>   EXAMPLE: The denotation of <u>skinny</u> is "very thin."
> ■ The **connotation** of a word is an added meaning that suggests something positive or negative.
>   EXAMPLES: **Negative:** <u>Skinny</u> suggests "too thin." Skinny has a negative connotation.
>   **Positive:** <u>Slender</u> suggests "attractively thin." Slender has a positive connotation.
> ■ Some words are neutral. They do not suggest either good or bad feelings.
>   EXAMPLES: month, building, chair

A. Underline the word in parentheses that has the more positive connotation.

1. Our trip to the amusement park was (fine, wonderful).

2. (Brave, Foolhardy) people rode on the roller coaster.

3. We saw (fascinating, weird) animals in the animal house.

4. Some of the monkeys made (hilarious, amusing) faces.

5. Everyone had a (smile, smirk) on his or her face on the way home.

B. Underline the word in parentheses that has the more negative connotation.

1. We bought (cheap, inexpensive) souvenirs at the amusement park.

2. I ate a (soggy, moist) sandwich.

3. Mike (nagged, reminded) us to go to the funny house.

4. The funny house was (comical, silly).

5. I didn't like the (smirk, grin) on the jester's face.

6. It made me feel (uneasy, frightened).

C. Answer the following questions.

1. Which is worth more, something <u>old</u> or something <u>antique</u>? _____

2. Is it better to be <u>slender</u> or to be <u>skinny</u>? _____

3. Which would you rather be called, <u>thrifty</u> or <u>cheap</u>? _____

4. Would a vain person be more likely to <u>stroll</u> or to <u>parade</u>? _____

5. Which is more serious, a <u>problem</u> or a <u>disaster</u>? _____

6. Is it more polite to <u>sip</u> a drink or to <u>gulp</u> it? _____

7. If you hadn't eaten for weeks, would you be <u>hungry</u> or <u>starving</u>? _____

8. After walking in mud, would your shoes be <u>dirty</u> or <u>filthy</u>? _____

Idioms

> ■ An **idiom** is an expression that has a meaning different from the usual meanings of the individual words within it.
> EXAMPLE: To lend a hand means "to help," not "to loan someone a hand."

A. Match the idioms underlined in the sentences below with their meanings. Write the correct letter on each line.

a. in a risky situation

b. do less than I should

c. admit having said the wrong thing

d. play music after only hearing it

e. spend money carefully

f. continue to have hope

g. listen with all your attention

h. teasing

i. accept defeat

j. meet by chance

_____ 1. I had hoped to run across some old friends at the ball game.

_____ 2. Their team was ready to throw in the towel when we scored our tenth run!

_____ 3. Peggy was pulling my leg when she told me that there are koala bears in Africa.

_____ 4. I told her that she was skating on thin ice when she tried to trick me.

_____ 5. My sister must make ends meet with the little money she has for college.

_____ 6. I told her, "Always keep your chin up when things get difficult."

_____ 7. José can play by ear the theme songs to all his favorite movies.

_____ 8. If you don't believe me, just be all ears when he plays.

_____ 9. My brother said that I would lie down on the job if he weren't watching over me.

_____ 10. I told Bill that he would eat his words once he saw how much work I had done.

B. Underline the idioms in the following sentences. On the line after each sentence, explain what the idiom means. Use a dictionary if necessary.

1. Frank was in hot water when he arrived late.

_____

2. His friends were beside themselves with worry.

_____

3. Frank told them not to fly off the handle.

_____

4. His friends explained that they had been shaken up.

_____

5. They all decided to sit down and talk turkey.

_____

Unit 1 Test

Choose whether the underlined words in each sentence are synonyms, antonyms, homonyms, or homographs.

1. If you duck your head under here, you can see the baby duck.

    A ○ synonyms   **B** ○ antonyms   **C** ○ homonyms   **D** ○ homographs

2. Please show me how to operate the lawn mower, so I can use it properly.

    A ○ synonyms   **B** ○ antonyms   **C** ○ homonyms   **D** ○ homographs

3. My friend asked me a question, but I told him I didn't know the answer.

    A ○ synonyms   **B** ○ antonyms   **C** ○ homonyms   **D** ○ homographs

4. The perfume she sent has a wonderful scent.

    A ○ synonyms   **B** ○ antonyms   **C** ○ homonyms   **D** ○ homographs

5. Don't worry about something that's not real; nothing will come of it.

    A ○ synonyms   **B** ○ antonyms   **C** ○ homonyms   **D** ○ homographs

6. Even though its leg is hurt, it's not broken.

    A ○ synonyms   **B** ○ antonyms   **C** ○ homonyms   **D** ○ homographs

7. Can you reach that can of peaches on the top shelf?

    A ○ synonyms   **B** ○ antonyms   **C** ○ homonyms   **D** ○ homographs

8. The brave soldiers won their battle, and they won medals for their fearless deeds.

    A ○ synonyms   **B** ○ antonyms   **C** ○ homonyms   **D** ○ homographs

9. They're going to their cabin for vacation.

    A ○ synonyms   **B** ○ antonyms   **C** ○ homonyms   **D** ○ homographs

10. Before you begin the next topic, please let me finish taking notes on this one.

    A ○ synonyms   **B** ○ antonyms   **C** ○ homonyms   **D** ○ homographs

Add a prefix or suffix to the underlined word to make a new word that makes sense in the sentence.

11. It is possible to sleep in at my house.

    A ○ pre-   **C** ○ im-
    B ○ un-   **D** ○ -ity

12. We spend end hours talking together.

    A ○ un-   **C** ○ -ful
    B ○ -less   **D** ○ -ous

13. Please move your shoes before entering.

    A ○ un-   **C** ○ -y
    B ○ -able   **D** ○ re-

14. Be care not to disturb the baby.

    A ○ -ful   **C** ○ -able
    B ○ -less   **D** ○ mis-

15. The train traveled <u>stop</u> to Chicago.

    A ○ dis-   **C** ○ non-
    B ○ -able   **D** ○ mis-

16. She had a <u>remark</u> way of explaining.

    A ○ un-   **C** ○ -ness
    B ○ -able   **D** ○ mis-

17. That country is very <u>mountain</u>.

    A ○ -al   **C** ○ -able
    B ○ -ness   **D** ○ -ous

18. He <u>placed</u> his new hat.

    A ○ un-   **C** ○ non-
    B ○ mis-   **D** ○ -able

19. We enjoyed the movie <u>view</u>.

    A ○ -al   **C** ○ pre-
    B ○ dis-   **D** ○ un-

20. We take an <u>occasion</u> trip.

    A ○ -al   **C** ○ un-
    B ○ -ous   **D** ○ -y

Choose the correct contraction for each pair of underlined words.

21. <u>you would</u>

    A ○ you'd   **C** ○ y'oud
    B ○ you'ld   **D** ○ youd'

22. <u>they are</u>

    A ○ there   **C** ○ theyr'e
    B ○ their   **D** ○ they're

23. <u>it is</u>

    A ○ its'   **C** ○ ites
    B ○ it's   **D** ○ its

24. <u>will not</u>

    A ○ win't   **C** ○ won't
    B ○ wo'nt   **D** ○ willn't

25. <u>I will</u>

    A ○ I'm   **C** ○ I'll
    B ○ I've   **D** ○ I'd

26. <u>does not</u>

    A ○ didn't   **C** ○ don't
    B ○ doesn't   **D** ○ does'nt

Add a word to each underlined word to make it a compound word.

27. We took the <u>ferry</u> to the island.

    A ○ tale   **C** ○ man
    B ○ boat   **D** ○ route

28. She could not <u>stand</u> him.

    A ○ by   **C** ○ grand
    B ○ head   **D** ○ under

Choose whether each underlined word has a positive connotation (+), a negative connotation (−), or is neutral (N).

29. This dress is <u>cheap</u>.   **A** ○ (+) **B** ○ (−) **C** ○ (N)

30. My sister is very <u>slender</u>.   **A** ○ (+) **B** ○ (−) **C** ○ (N)

31. Tom will <u>walk</u> with us.   **A** ○ (+) **B** ○ (−) **C** ○ (N)

32. The movie was <u>disgusting</u>.   **A** ○ (+) **B** ○ (−) **C** ○ (N)

33. The heroine was <u>brave</u>.   **A** ○ (+) **B** ○ (−) **C** ○ (N)

34. Did you ask your <u>doctor</u>?   **A** ○ (+) **B** ○ (−) **C** ○ (N)

Choose the correct meaning for each idiom.

35. beside herself

    A ○ out of favor

    B ○ very upset

    C ○ unable to decide

    D ○ in a difficult situation

36. walking on air

    A ○ accept defeat

    B ○ extremely happy

    C ○ meet by chance

    D ○ be in trouble

Recognizing Sentences

> ■ A **sentence** is a group of words that expresses a complete thought.
> EXAMPLE: Marie sings well.

■ **Some of the following groups of words are sentences, and some are not. Write** <u>S</u> **before each group that is a sentence. Punctuate each sentence with a period.**

_____ 1. When the downhill skiing season begins____

_____ 2. Last summer I visited my friend in New Jersey____

_____ 3. From the very beginning of the first-aid lessons____

_____ 4. One of the children from the neighborhood____

_____ 5. A visiting musician played the organ____

_____ 6. On the way to school this morning____

_____ 7. "I love you, Mother," said Mike____

_____ 8. The blue house at the corner of Maple Street____

_____ 9. After Emily left, the phone rang off the hook____

_____ 10. Speak distinctly and loudly so that you can be heard____

_____ 11. I have finally learned to drive our car____

_____ 12. This is William's tenth birthday____

_____ 13. At the very last moment, we were ready____

_____ 14. When you speak in front of people____

_____ 15. The basket of fruit on the table____

_____ 16. Please answer the telephone, Julia____

_____ 17. Hurrying to class because he is late____

_____ 18. The first thing in the morning____

_____ 19. That mistake was costly and unfortunate____

_____ 20. We are planning to build a new doghouse____

_____ 21. The dog chased the cat up the tree____

_____ 22. Daniel Boone was born in Pennsylvania____

_____ 23. The giant cottonwood in our backyard____

_____ 24. Marla, bring my notebook____

_____ 25. On a stool beside the back door____

_____ 26. Sometimes the noise from the street____

_____ 27. Somewhere out of state____

_____ 28. The band played a lively march____

_____ 29. That flight arrived on time____

_____ 30. Was cracked in dozens of places____

Name _____   Date _____

Types of Sentences

- A **declarative** sentence makes a statement. It is followed by a
  period (.).   EXAMPLES: It is warm today. I took off my coat.
- An **interrogative** sentence asks a question. It is followed by a question
  mark (?).   EXAMPLES: When is Tony coming? Why is the bus late today?

- Write **D** before each declarative sentence and **IN** before each interrogative sentence.
  Put the correct punctuation mark at the end of the sentence.

____IN____ **1.** Who is your favorite author_?_

_____ **2.** How are our forests protected from fire____

_____ **3.** Tim learned the names of the trees in his neighborhood____

_____ **4.** A good driver obeys every traffic law____

_____ **5.** The hippopotamus lives in Africa____

_____ **6.** Do you know the legend of the dogwood tree____

_____ **7.** Every sentence should begin with a capital letter____

_____ **8.** Ryan is repairing the lamp____

_____ **9.** Did you ever see a kangaroo____

_____ **10.** Where did these fragrant roses grow____

_____ **11.** Beautiful furniture can be made from the oak tree____

_____ **12.** Flour can be made from dried bananas____

_____ **13.** Did anyone find Steve's book____

_____ **14.** Andrea feeds the goldfish every day____

_____ **15.** How many people are studying to be pilots____

_____ **16.** Kelly is going to the show with us____

_____ **17.** Last summer we made a trip to Carlsbad Caverns____

_____ **18.** How old are you____

_____ **19.** The architect and her assistant inspected the building____

_____ **20.** When did you arrive at the meeting____

_____ **21.** Did you forget your wallet____

_____ **22.** That light bulb is burned out____

_____ **23.** The baby crawled across the room____

_____ **24.** When would you like to eat____

_____ **25.** Jo helped Andy wash the car____

_____ **26.** Did they wax the car____

_____ **27.** How did you make that sand castle____

_____ **28.** It is easy to make if we work together____

More Types of Sentences

> - An **imperative** sentence expresses a command or a request. It is followed by a period (.).   EXAMPLE: Close the door.
> - An **exclamatory** sentence expresses strong or sudden feeling. It is followed by an exclamation point (!).   EXAMPLE: I am innocent!

■ Write **IM** before each imperative sentence and **E** before each exclamatory sentence. Put the correct punctuation mark at the end of each sentence.

__IM__ 1. Write the names of the days of the week___.___

_____ 2. Please mail this package for me____

_____ 3. I love the gift you gave me____

_____ 4. Lay the papers on the desk____

_____ 5. How beautiful the night is____

_____ 6. Watch out for that turning car____

_____ 7. Drive more slowly____

_____ 8. Keep time with the music____

_____ 9. Deliver this message immediately____

_____ 10. Sign your name in my yearbook____

_____ 11. That airplane is so huge____

_____ 12. Please lend me a postage stamp____

_____ 13. I'm delighted with the flowers____

_____ 14. How blue the sky is____

_____ 15. My neighbor's shed is on fire____

_____ 16. The baby's lip is bleeding____

_____ 17. I can't believe that I got a perfect score____

_____ 18. Pass the green beans____

_____ 19. Write down these sentences____

_____ 20. That movie was so exciting____

_____ 21. The puppy is so playful____

_____ 22. Look both ways when crossing the street____

_____ 23. What a pretty red and blue sailboat____

_____ 24. Please repeat what you said____

_____ 25. Put the vase on the table____

_____ 26. Be more careful with your work____

_____ 27. That's a fantastic book to read____

_____ 28. This is a wonderful surprise____

Complete Subjects and Predicates

> - Every sentence has two main parts, a **complete subject** and a **complete predicate**.
> - The complete subject includes all the words that tell who or what the sentence is about.
>   EXAMPLES: **My brother**/likes to go with us. **Six geese**/honked loudly.
> - The complete predicate includes all the words that state the action or condition of the subject.
>   EXAMPLES: My brother/**likes to go with us**. Six geese/**honked loudly**.

- **Draw a line between the complete subject and the complete predicate in each sentence.**

1. Bees/fly.
2. Trains whistle.
3. A talented artist drew this cartoon.
4. The wind blew furiously.
5. My grandmother made this dress last year.
6. We surely have enjoyed the holiday.
7. These cookies are made with rice.
8. This letter came to the post office box.
9. They rent a cabin in Colorado every summer.
10. Jennifer is reading about the pioneer days in the West.
11. Our baseball team won the third game of the series.
12. The band played a cheerful tune.
13. A cloudless sky is a great help to a pilot.
14. The voice of the auctioneer was heard throughout the hall.
15. A sudden flash of lightning startled us.
16. The wind howled down the chimney.
17. Paul's dog followed him to the grocery store.
18. Their apartment is on the sixth floor.
19. We have studied many interesting places.
20. Each player on the team deserves credit for the victory.
21. Forest rangers fought the raging fire.
22. A friend taught Robert a valuable lesson.
23. Millions of stars make up the Milky Way.
24. The airplane was lost in the thick clouds.
25. Many of the children waded in the pool.
26. Yellowstone Park is a large national park.
27. Cold weather is predicted for tomorrow.
28. The trees were covered with moss.

Name _____   Date _____

Simple Subjects and Predicates

> - The **simple subject** of a sentence is the main word in the complete subject. The simple subject is a noun or a word that stands for a noun.
>   EXAMPLE: My **sister**/lost her gloves.
> - Sometimes the simple subject is also the complete subject.
>   EXAMPLE: **She**/lost her gloves.
> - The **simple predicate** of a sentence is a verb within the complete predicate. The simple predicate may be a one-word verb or a verb of more than one word.
>   EXAMPLES: She/**lost** her gloves. She/**is looking** for them.

- **Draw a line between the complete subject and complete predicate in each sentence below. Underline the simple subject once and the simple predicate twice.**

1. A sudden clap of thunder/frightened all of us.

2. The soft snow covered the fields and roads.

3. We drove very slowly over the narrow bridge.

4. The students are making an aquarium.

5. Our class read about the founder of Hull House.

6. The women were talking in the park.

7. This album has many folk songs.

8. We are furnishing the sandwiches for tonight's picnic.

9. All the trees on that lawn are giant oaks.

10. Many Americans are working in foreign countries.

11. The manager read the names of the contest winners.

12. Bill brought these large melons.

13. We opened the front door of the house.

14. The two mechanics worked on the car for an hour.

15. Black and yellow butterflies fluttered among the flowers.

16. The child spoke politely.

17. We found many beautiful shells along the shore.

18. The best part of the program is the dance number.

19. Every ambitious person is working hard.

20. Sheryl swam across the lake two times.

21. Our program will begin promptly at eight o'clock.

22. The handle of this basket is broken.

23. The clock in the tower strikes every hour.

24. The white farmhouse on that road belongs to my cousin.

25. The first game of the season will be played tomorrow.

Subjects and Predicates in Inverted Order

- When the subject of a sentence comes before all or part of the predicate, the sentence is in **natural order.**
  EXAMPLE: The <u>puppy</u> <u>scampered</u> away.
- When all or part of the predicate comes before the subject, the sentence is in **inverted order.**
  EXAMPLE: Away <u>scampered</u> the <u>puppy</u>.
- Many interrogative sentences are in inverted order.
  EXAMPLE: Where <u>is</u>/<u>James</u>?

A. Draw a line between the complete subject and the complete predicate in each sentence. Write <u>I</u> in front of sentences that are in inverted order.

_____I_____ 1. Lightly falls/the mist.

_____ 2. The peaches on this tree are ripe now.

_____ 3. Over and over rolled the rocks.

_____ 4. Down the street marched the band.

_____ 5. Near the ocean are many birds.

_____ 6. Right under the chair ran the kitten.

_____ 7. He hit the ball a long way.

_____ 8. Along the ridge hiked the campers.

_____ 9. Underground is the stream.

_____ 10. The fish jumped in the lake.

_____ 11. Over the hill came the trucks.

_____ 12. Out came the rainbow.

B. Rewrite each inverted sentence in Exercise A in natural order.

1. _____

2. _____

3. _____

4. _____

5. _____

6. _____

7. _____

8. _____

9. _____

Using Compound Subjects

> ■ Two sentences in which the subjects are different but the predicates are the same can be combined into one sentence. The two subjects are joined by <u>and</u>. The subject of the new sentence is called a **compound subject.**
>
>   EXAMPLE: **Lynn** visited an amusement park.
>   **Eric** visited an amusement park.
>   **Lynn and Eric** visited an amusement park.

A. Draw a line between the complete subject and the complete predicate in each sentence. If the subject is compound, write <u>CS</u> before the sentence.

__CS__   1. English settlers and Spanish settlers/came to North America in the 1600s.

_____   2. Trees and bushes were chopped down to make room for their houses.

_____   3. The fierce winds and the cold temperatures made the first winters very harsh.

_____   4. The settlers and Native Americans became friends.

_____   5. Native Americans helped the settlers grow food in the new country.

_____   6. Potatoes and corn were first grown by Native Americans.

_____   7. English settlers and Spanish settlers had never tasted turkey.

_____   8. Peanuts and sunflower seeds are Native American foods that we now eat for snacks.

_____   9. Lima beans and corn are combined to make succotash.

_____ 10. Zucchini is an American squash that was renamed by Italian settlers.

_____ 11. Native Americans also introduced barbecuing to the settlers.

B. Combine each pair of sentences below. Underline the compound subject.

1. Gold from the New World was sent to Spain. Silver from the New World was sent to Spain.

_____

_____

2. France staked claims in the Americas in the 1500s and 1600s. The Netherlands staked claims in the Americas in the 1500s and 1600s.

_____

_____

3. John Cabot explored areas of the Americas. Henry Hudson explored areas of the Americas.

_____

_____

C. Write a sentence with a compound subject.

_____

Using Compound Predicates

> ■ Two sentences in which the subjects are the same but the predicates
> are different can be combined into one sentence. The two predicates
> may be joined by <u>or</u>, <u>and</u>, or <u>but</u>. The predicate of the new sentence is
> called a **compound predicate.**
>   EXAMPLE: The crowd **cheered** the players.
>   The crowd **applauded** the players.
>   The crowd **cheered and applauded** the players.

**A. Draw a line between the complete subject and the complete predicate in each
sentence. If the predicate is compound, write <u>CP</u> before the sentence.**

_____ **1.** The students organized a picnic for their families.

_____ **2.** They discussed and chose a date for the picnic.

_____ **3.** They wrote and designed invitations.

_____ **4.** The invitations were mailed and delivered promptly.

_____ **5.** Twenty-five families responded to the invitations.

_____ **6.** The students bought the food and made the sandwiches.

_____ **7.** The families bought the soft drinks.

_____ **8.** The students packed and loaded the food into a truck.

_____ **9.** The families brought and set up the volleyball nets.

_____ **10.** Everyone participated in the games and races.

_____ **11.** They ran relay races and threw water balloons.

_____ **12.** Everyone packed the food and cleaned up the picnic area at the end of the day.

B. Combine each pair of sentences below. Underline the compound predicate.

1. Caroline heard the music. Caroline memorized the music.

_____

_____

2. Keith picked up the newspapers. Keith loaded the newspapers into his car.

_____

_____

3. Larry studied the names of the states. Larry wrote down the names of the states.

_____

_____

C. Write a sentence with a compound predicate.

_____

_____

Name _____   Date _____

Simple and Compound Sentences

- A **simple sentence** has one subject and one predicate.
  EXAMPLE: The earth/is covered by land and water.
- A **compound sentence** is made up of two simple sentences joined by a connecting word such as <u>and</u>, <u>but</u>, and <u>or</u>. A comma is placed before the connecting word.
  EXAMPLE: One-fourth of the earth/is covered by land, and the land/is divided into seven continents.

A. Draw a line between the complete subject and the complete predicate in each sentence. Write <u>S</u> before each simple sentence. Write <u>C</u> before each compound sentence.

_____ 1. The seven continents of the world are North America, South America, Africa, Europe, Australia, Asia, and Antarctica.

_____ 2. Three-fourths of the earth is covered by water, and most of it is salty ocean water.

_____ 3. The four oceans of the world are the Pacific, the Atlantic, the Indian, and the Arctic.

_____ 4. We cannot exist without water, but we cannot drink the salty ocean water.

_____ 5. Most of the water we drink comes from lakes, rivers, and streams.

_____ 6. Clean water is a priceless resource.

B. Combine each pair of simple sentences below into a compound sentence.

1. The Pacific Ocean is the largest ocean in the world.
   It covers more area than all the earth's land put together.

   _____

   _____

2. Bodies of saltwater that are smaller than oceans are called seas, gulfs, or bays.
   These bodies of water are often encircled by land.

   _____

   _____

3. Seas, gulfs, and bays are joined to the oceans.
   They vary in size and depth.

   _____

   _____

4. The Mediterranean is one of the earth's largest seas.
   It is almost entirely encircled by the southern part of Europe, the northern part of Africa, and the western part of Asia.

   _____

   _____

   _____

Correcting Run–on Sentences

- Two or more sentences run together without the correct punctuation are called a **run-on sentence.**
  - EXAMPLE: It will rain today, it will be sunny tomorrow.
- One way to correct a run-on sentence is to separate it into two sentences.
  - EXAMPLE: It will rain today. It will be sunny tomorrow.
- Another way to correct a run-on sentence is to separate the two main parts with a comma and <u>and</u>, <u>or</u>, <u>but</u>, <u>nor</u>, or <u>yet</u>.
  - EXAMPLE: It will rain today, but it will be sunny tomorrow.

- **Rewrite each run-on sentence correctly.**

1. In 1860, the Pony Express started in St. Joseph, Missouri the route began where the railroads ended.

_____

_____

2. People in the West wanted faster mail service, the mail took six weeks by boat.

_____

_____

3. Mail sent by stagecoach took about 21 days, the Pony Express averaged ten days.

_____

_____

4. The Pony Express used a relay system riders and horses were switched at 157 places along the way to Sacramento, California.

_____

_____

5. Because teenagers weighed less than adults, most of the riders were teenagers the horses could run faster carrying them.

_____

_____

6. Riders had to cross raging rivers, the mountains were another barrier.

_____

_____

Name _____   Date _____

Expanding Sentences

- Sentences can be **expanded** by adding details to make them clearer and more interesting.
  EXAMPLE: The child waved. The child **in the blue hat** waved **timidly to me.**
- Details added to sentences may answer these questions: When? (today) Where? (at home) How? (slowly) How often? (daily) To what degree? (very) What kind? (big) Which? (smallest) How many? (five)

A. Expand each sentence by adding details to answer the questions shown in parentheses. Write the expanded sentence on the line.

1. The ball soared.   (What kind? Where?)

   _____

2. It crashed.   (How? Where?)

   _____

3. It rolled.   (When? Where?)

   _____

4. I felt.   (How? To what degree?)

   _____

B. Decide how each of the following sentences can be expanded. Write your new sentence on the line.

1. The fires spread. _____

   _____

2. People ran. _____

   _____

3. Homes and trees blazed. _____

   _____

4. Firefighters came. _____

   _____

5. Water sprayed. _____

   _____

6. Flames died out. _____

   _____

Unit 2 Test

Choose the phrase that is not a sentence.

1. **A** ○ Here we go!

   B ○ Having fun now.

   C ○ Let's go eat.

   D ○ Will you come?

2. **A** ○ In a minute.

   B ○ She was sleeping.

   C ○ The storm ended.

   D ○ Don't go alone.

3. **A** ○ You should see that!

   B ○ Why are you here?

   C ○ Do the right thing.

   D ○ For my friend.

4. **A** ○ He said nothing.

   B ○ It was old.

   C ○ Fine for her.

   D ○ The dog barked.

Choose (A) if the group of words is an interrogative sentence, (B) if it is an imperative sentence, (C) if it is an exclamatory sentence, or (D) if it is a declarative sentence.

5. Be careful with that. **A** ○ **B** ○ **C** ○ **D** ○

6. When did you go? **A** ○ **B** ○ **C** ○ **D** ○

7. Why did you leave? **A** ○ **B** ○ **C** ○ **D** ○

8. What a wonderful **A** ○ **B** ○ **C** ○ **D** ○
   day it is!

9. I must show her. **A** ○ **B** ○ **C** ○ **D** ○

10. Don't drop that. **A** ○ **B** ○ **C** ○ **D** ○

11. Would they come? **A** ○ **B** ○ **C** ○ **D** ○

12. Be there by noon. **A** ○ **B** ○ **C** ○ **D** ○

13. He is such a nice **A** ○ **B** ○ **C** ○ **D** ○
    person!

14. I'll go down by the **A** ○ **B** ○ **C** ○ **D** ○
    river.

15. I was so surprised! **A** ○ **B** ○ **C** ○ **D** ○

16. What did you say? **A** ○ **B** ○ **C** ○ **D** ○

Choose each sentence that has a line drawn between the complete subject and the complete predicate.

17. **A** ○ My sister Claire/likes to swim in the lake
       before breakfast.

    B ○ Sam will/clean the fish that we catch today.

    C ○ My brother and sister are/cleaning the sailboat.

    D ○ Janice saw/Steven at the lake.

18. **A** ○ The seasons are the/four divisions of
       the year.

    B ○ The origin/of the wheat plant is uncertain.

    C ○ Yosemite National Park/is very popular.

    D ○ Many towns/in the United States are built
       near water.

19. **A** ○ I like to study/chemistry and biology.

    B ○ My sister/graduated from college last year.

    C ○ Many/tourists visit Paris, France, each year.

    D ○ The railroad passes through/the middle of
       the city.

20. **A** ○ My friends and I went to/London last
       summer.

    B ○ The doctor said it's/nothing to worry about.

    C ○ I really like the/new computer you bought.

    D ○ Pamela/has been sick for three days.

Choose the sentence in which the simple subject is underlined.

21. **A** ○ They caught all <u>kinds</u> of fish.

    B ○ My <u>dog</u> has fleas.

    C ○ <u>This</u> is my favorite tool.

    D ○ <u>Her</u> only brother is visiting.

22. **A** ○ The warm <u>climate</u> attracts visitors.

    B ○ The people <u>boarded</u> a train.

    C ○ The tall <u>pine</u> trees hid the cabin.

    D ○ She filled the <u>vase</u> with flowers.

Choose the sentence in which the simple predicate is underlined.

23. **A** ○ Jerry <u>closed</u> the store early.

    B ○ Karen <u>has been</u> on vacation.

    C ○ Jacob <u>can</u> play the flute.

    D ○ We <u>saw</u> them yesterday.

24. **A** ○ She <u>spoke</u> politely.

    B ○ The first game will <u>be</u> tomorrow.

    C ○ Our program <u>is</u> starting soon.

    D ○ The handle <u>broke</u> in half.

Choose the sentence that is in inverted order.

25. **A** ○ Down came the rain.

    B ○ She fell on the ice.

    C ○ The cat scratched the chair.

    D ○ The judge is coming.

26. **A** ○ Tell me about it.

    B ○ How did that happen?

    C ○ We went up the stairs.

    D ○ The dish fell and broke.

Choose the sentence that has a compound subject.

27. **A** ○ Fred went fishing and hiking.

    B ○ The boys waded out into the stream.

    C ○ Carla and Rudy cooked dinner.

    D ○ The storm howled and raged.

Choose the sentence that has a compound predicate.

28. **A** ○ She made and wrapped all her presents.

    B ○ The clerk added up the numbers.

    C ○ He turned around slowly.

    D ○ Thirty men and women enrolled.

Choose the sentence that is a compound sentence.

29. **A** ○ I would like to go, but I can't.

    B ○ Last night, we saw Pete and Sara at the movie theater.

    C ○ Jane and Josie will help Zachary wash the car tomorrow.

    D ○ Would you like fish or chicken for lunch, Ladonna?

30. **A** ○ Yes, I prefer to go home.

    B ○ She wanted to go to the first game of the season.

    C ○ You can go with him, or you can stay with me.

    D ○ Since when do you like to watch football?

Choose the sentence that is a run-on sentence.

31. **A** ○ My grandfather works as a janitor at a hospital.

    B ○ He enjoys working with his hands, and he likes to meet new people.

    C ○ He once fixed our furnace, it's worked well ever since.

    D ○ My mom says that I got my common sense from Grandpa.

32. **A** ○ Have you ever seen the Statue of Liberty, it's in New York?

    B ○ The statue is copper, and it was given to the U.S. by France in 1884.

    C ○ The statue's official name is Liberty Enlightening the World.

    D ○ Each year, approximately two million people visit the Statue of Liberty.

Nouns

> ■ A **noun** is a word that names a person, place, thing, or quality.
> EXAMPLES: boy, Maria, river, Wyoming, house, beach, joy

A. Write nouns that name the following:

1. Four famous people

_____   _____

_____   _____

2. Four types of jobs

_____   _____

_____   _____

3. Four places you would like to visit

_____   _____

_____   _____

4. Four vegetables

_____   _____

_____   _____

5. Four qualities you would like to possess

_____   _____

_____   _____

B. Underline each noun.

1. Alaska is rich in gold, silver, copper, and oil.
2. Chocolate is made from the beans of a tree that grows in the tropics.
3. The distance across Texas is greater than the distance from Chicago to New York.
4. The men and women rode their horses in the parade.
5. The oldest city in California is San Diego.
6. Alexander Graham Bell, the inventor of the telephone, was born in Edinburgh, Scotland.
7. Jack, Diane, and I took a plane to London, where we saw Buckingham Palace.
8. Many interesting animals, such as piranhas, alligators, anacondas, and sloths, live in the Amazon River Basin.
9. The tarantula is a type of large, hairy spider.
10. The Maya were a people who lived in what is now Mexico and Central America.

Name _____   Date _____

Common and Proper Nouns

- There are two main types of nouns: **common nouns** and **proper nouns**.
- A **common noun** names any one of a class of objects.
    EXAMPLES: girl, state, author
- A **proper noun** is the name of a particular person, place, or thing. A proper noun begins with a capital letter.
    EXAMPLES: Mark Twain, Tennessee, Washington Monument

A. Write a proper noun suggested by each common noun.

1. college _____   11. car _____
2. river _____   12. school _____
3. governor _____   13. lake _____
4. singer _____   14. country _____
5. physician _____   15. street _____
6. holiday _____   16. park _____
7. TV show _____   17. month _____
8. city _____   18. actor _____
9. teacher _____   19. girl _____
10. classmate _____   20. state _____

B. Write a common noun suggested by each proper noun.

1. Alaska _____   11. Mars _____
2. South America _____   12. Bill Clinton _____
3. Tuesday _____   13. February _____
4. Nile _____   14. Andes Mountains _____
5. Dr. Washington _____   15. Mexico _____
6. Lake Superior _____   16. *Treasure Island* _____
7. Thanksgiving _____   17. Jennifer _____
8. Pacific _____   18. Paris _____
9. Arizona _____   19. Washington, D.C. _____
10. David _____   20. Fido _____

C. Underline each common noun.

1. The sturdy timber of the oak is used in constructing furniture, bridges, and ships.

2. Robert Fulton was a painter, jeweler, farmer, engineer, and inventor.

3. The main crops of Puerto Rico are sugar, tobacco, coffee, and fruits.

4. The pecan groves of Texas provide nuts for the eastern part of the United States.

5. France has many rivers and beaches.

6. The Verrazano-Narrows Bridge between Brooklyn and Staten Island is the longest suspension bridge in the world.

7. Some of the main foods eaten in Greece are lamb, fish, olives, and feta cheese.

8. A road passes through a tunnel cut in the base of a giant tree in California.

9. Since the earliest civilizations, gold has been used for ornaments.

10. One of the largest lakes in North America is Lake Erie.

11. The orange tree bears beautiful blossoms and delicious fruits.

12. Rockefeller Center is a large business and entertainment center in New York.

13. Pine trees give us turpentine, tar, resin, timber, and oils.

14. The United States buys the greatest amount of the world's coffee.

15. The pelican, the penguin, and the flamingo are interesting birds.

16. The first trip into space was filled with danger.

D. Underline each proper noun.

1. The principal goods exported by Brazil are soybeans, sugar, and coffee.

2. William Penn was the founder of Pennsylvania.

3. On the shelves of the Elm Grove Library, you will find many magical stories.

4. Commander Byrd, a naval officer, made the first airplane flight to the North Pole.

5. Dr. Jeanne Spurlock went to Howard University College of Medicine.

6. The orange tree was brought to Europe from Asia.

7. Colombia is the world's leading producer of emeralds.

8. Kilimanjaro is the tallest mountain in Africa.

9. The Navajo make beautiful silver and turquoise jewelry.

10. Leticia and Carlos anchored the tent while Sam and Ted prepared the food.

11. Thomas Jefferson introduced the decimal system of coinage (dollars, dimes, cents) that is now used in the United States.

12. Their home is on the shore of Lake Michigan.

13. Quebec is the only city in North America that has a wall around it.

14. Paul Revere was a patriot, a silversmith, an engraver, and a dentist.

15. Lemons were first grown in the valleys of India.

16. The Sears Tower in Chicago is the tallest building in the world.

Singular and Plural Nouns

- A **singular noun** names one person, place, or thing.
  EXAMPLES: girl, half, pear, sky
- A **plural noun** names more than one person, place, or thing.
  EXAMPLES: girls, halves, pears, skies
- Add -s to most nouns to make them plural.
  EXAMPLES: girl, girls   top, tops
- Add -es to most nouns ending in -ch, -sh, -s, or -x to make them plural.
  EXAMPLES: church, churches   brush, brushes   ax, axes
- If a noun ends in a consonant and -y, change the -y to -i and add -es.
  EXAMPLES: city, cities   army, armies
- If a noun ends in a vowel and -y, add -s to make it plural.
  EXAMPLE: boy, boys

A. Write the plural form for each noun below.

1. newspaper _____

2. guess _____

3. town _____

4. valley _____

5. body _____

6. story _____

7. bush _____

8. office _____

9. tax _____

10. toy _____

11. boss _____

12. school _____

13. day _____

14. copy _____

15. author _____

16. porch _____

B. Complete each sentence with the plural form of the noun in parentheses.

1. (penny) How many _____ make a dollar?

2. (dress) Marcy makes all of her own_____.

3. (bridge) How many _____ were destroyed by the flood?

4. (brush) Mr. Perez got two new _____ yesterday.

5. (county) How many _____ are there in your state?

6. (fox) Seven _____ live at the zoo.

7. (book) I like to read _____ about our pioneers.

8. (lunch) She made several _____ before school.

9. (country) How many _____ are there in South America?

Name _____   Date _____

- Some nouns ending in -f or -fe are made plural by changing the -f or -fe to -ves.
    EXAMPLES: loaf, loaves   wife, wives
- Some nouns ending in -f are made plural by adding -s.
    EXAMPLES: roof, roofs   bluff, bluffs
- Most nouns ending in -o that have a vowel just before the -o are made plural by adding -s.
    EXAMPLE: radio, radios
- Some nouns ending in -o preceded by a consonant are made plural by adding -es, but others are made plural by adding only -s.
    EXAMPLES: potato, potatoes   piano, pianos
- A few nouns have irregular plural forms.
    EXAMPLES: child, children   man, men   ox, oxen
- A few nouns have the same form for both the singular and plural.
    EXAMPLES: trout, trout   sheep, sheep

C. Write the plural form for each noun below. You might wish to check the spellings in a dictionary.

1. knife _____

2. loaf _____

3. half _____

4. mouse _____

5. foot _____

6. goose _____

7. hoof _____

8. moose _____

9. life _____

10. tomato _____

11. tooth _____

12. piano _____

D. Complete each sentence with the plural form of the word in parentheses. You may wish to check the spellings in a dictionary.

1. (foot)   My new shoes pinch my _____.

2. (sheep)   The shepherd always takes good care of the _____.

3. (chimney)   Many _____ were blown down during the recent storm.

4. (city)   Many _____ are establishing recreation centers.

5. (leaf)   The high winds scattered the dead _____ over the yard.

6. (Mosquito)   _____ breed wherever there is standing water.

7. (nickel)   I have five Jefferson _____.

8. (friend)   Her _____ arrived on the bus yesterday.

9. (desk)   New _____ have been ordered for our office.

10. (bench)   Concrete _____ have been placed along the walk.

Possessive Nouns

- A **possessive noun** shows possession of the noun that follows.
- Form the possessive of most singular nouns by adding an apostrophe (') and -s.
  EXAMPLES: the boy's hat   Mr. Thomas's car
- Form the possessive of a plural noun ending in -s by adding only an apostrophe.
  EXAMPLES: the Smiths' home   girls' bikes   sisters' names
- Form the possessive of a plural noun that does not end in -s by adding an apostrophe and -s.
  EXAMPLES: children's classes   men's books

A. Write the possessive form of each noun.

1. girl _____girl's_____   6. baby _____   11. brother _____

2. child _____   7. boys _____   12. soldier _____

3. women _____   8. teacher _____   13. men _____

4. children _____   9. Dr. Ray _____   14. aunt _____

5. John _____   10. ladies _____   15. Ms. Jones _____

B. Rewrite each phrase using a possessive noun.

1. the cap belonging to Jim _____Jim's cap_____

2. the wrench that belongs to Kathy _____

3. the smile of the baby _____

4. the car that my friend owns _____

5. the new shoes that belong to Kim _____

6. the collar of the dog _____

7. the golf clubs that Frank owns _____

8. the shoes that belong to the runners _____

9. the friends of our parents _____

10. the opinion of the editor _____

11. the lunches of the children _____

12. the coat belonging to Kyle _____

13. the assignment of the teacher _____

Name _____ Date _____

C. Complete each sentence with the possessive form of the word in parentheses.

1. (company) The _____ picnic will be at the park Saturday afternoon.

2. (dog) That _____ owner should pay for the damage it did.

3. (women) The _____ organization planned the meeting.

4. (Doug) _____ account of his trip was very interesting.

5. (David) _____ explanation of the problem was very clear.

6. (cat) My _____ eyes are blue.

7. (Kurt) _____ brother made the candy for our party.

8. (Men) _____ coats are sold at the store in that block.

9. (squirrel) The _____ teeth were very sharp.

10. (brother) We want to go to his _____ ranch.

11. (child) A _____ toy was found in our yard.

12. (calf) The _____ nose was soft and shiny.

13. (baby) That dog played with the _____ shoe.

14. (teachers) Her _____ names are Miss Gomez and Mr. Jacobs.

15. (Alex) We are going to _____ party tomorrow.

16. (deer) They saw a _____ tracks in the snow.

17. (Stacy) _____ work is the neatest I have ever seen.

18. (country) We display our _____ flag every day.

19. (robins) I have heard those _____ calls every day this week.

20. (person) That _____ speech was much too long.

21. (sister) Nichole wants to go to her _____ graduation.

22. (children) The _____ parade is held every spring.

23. (neighbors) Our _____ yards have just been mowed.

24. (class) It is this _____ time to take the test.

25. (boys) This store sells _____ clothes.

26. (designer) The _____ exhibit won first place.

27. (horse) The _____ mane is black.

Name _____   Date _____

Appositives

> ■ An **appositive** is a noun or phrase that identifies or explains the noun it follows.
> ■ Use a comma before and after an appositive. If an appositive is at the end of a sentence, use a comma before it.
>   EXAMPLES: Jenna is graduating from Spring Hill, **her junior high school.**
>   Christopher's baseball team, **the Padres,** won every game they played.

A. Circle the appositive in each sentence. Underline the noun it identifies or explains.

1. Henry, my father's older brother, drove trains.

2. His train, the Missouri Pacific, carried mostly freight.

3. Seattle, the location of the main station, was where the freight was loaded.

4. Coal and lumber, its main cargo, was then shipped east.

5. When Henry, our uncle, came to visit, we asked many questions.

6. He never tired of telling us, his nephews, about his life.

7. Uncle Henry would joke with my father, his brother, and they laughed a great deal.

8. Uncle Henry would tease my mother, his sister-in-law, too.

9. We especially liked it when he brought Aunt Emma, his wife, with him.

10. It was nice to see our cousins, Todd and Elizabeth, too.

B. Write sentences using the appositives below.

1. the cleanest room in the house ___Our living room, the cleanest room in the house, is___ ___usually kept for entertaining company.___

2. the most interesting subject _____

_____

3. the best day of the week _____

_____

4. my favorite sport _____

_____

5. a movie star _____

_____

6. a tropical island _____

_____

Name _____   Date _____

Verbs

> ■ A **verb** is a word that expresses action, being, or state of being.
> EXAMPLES: Helen **went** to school. These books **are** yours.
> Elizabeth and Paul **sing** in the choir.

■ **Underline the verb in each sentence.**

1. Where are the Alps?
2. W. C. Handy wrote "Saint Louis Blues."
3. Check your papers carefully.
4. Bananas have great food value.
5. Africa is the home of the hippopotamus.
6. The car reached the narrow bridge.
7. Gwendolyn Brooks won a Pulitzer Prize.
8. Elizabeth's father trains good mechanics.
9. Sue has a black puppy.
10. How many stars are on the United States flag?
11. The people of our town remember the cold winter.
12. Peter Minuit bought Manhattan Island for about twenty-four dollars.
13. What is your favorite book?
14. They followed the old trail to the top of the hill.
15. The wind whistled around the corner.
16. Eric always watches the news.
17. Their team scored twice in the third quarter.
18. Which driver won the auto race?
19. The third house from the corner is white.
20. Mexico lays to the south of the United States.
21. Tom set the table for five people.
22. Answer my question.
23. Lucy explained the operation of the computer.
24. Jason worked in the flower bed for his neighbor.
25. Our town has a public swimming pool.
26. My brother plays the saxophone.
27. Brush your teeth frequently.
28. A puff of wind whirled the leaves over the lawn.
29. We arrived at our camp early in the morning.
30. Where is the launching pad?

Verb Phrases

> - Some sentences contain a **verb phrase**. A verb phrase consists of a
>   **main verb** and one or more other verbs.
>   EXAMPLES: The women **are singing**. Where **have** you **been**?

- **Underline the verb or verb phrase in each sentence.**

1. The first American schools were held in homes.

2. Who invented the jet engine?

3. *The New England Primer* was the earliest United States textbook.

4. John Philip Sousa was a bandmaster and composer.

5. Who built the first motorcycle?

6. My friends will arrive on Saturday afternoon.

7. What was the final score?

8. Ryan has made this unusual birdhouse.

9. The waves covered the beach with many shells.

10. I have ridden on a motor scooter.

11. The artist is molding clay.

12. Beverly and her friends spent last summer in the mountains.

13. The names of the new employees are posted by the supervisor.

14. Paul has found a new hat.

15. She is going to the store.

16. We have trimmed the hedges.

17. The United States exports many kinds of food.

18. My friend is reading a book about World War I.

19. Jane Addams helped many foreign-born people in Chicago, Illinois.

20. Oil was discovered in many parts of North America.

21. Jenny Lind was called the Swedish Nightingale.

22. We are planning a car trip to Miami, Florida.

23. That dog has howled for two hours.

24. Our guests have arrived.

25. I have written letters to several companies.

26. I can name two important cities in that country.

27. The hummingbird received its name because of the sound of its wings.

28. Jan's poem was printed in the newspaper.

29. Charles and Adam are working at the hamburger stand.

30. This table was painted recently.

Helping Verbs

- The last word of a verb phrase is the main verb. The other words are **helping verbs.**

                    helping verb   main verb
                         ↓   ↓
    EXAMPLES: Beth and Jon **were** **sitting** on the bench.
                  Apples **are** **displayed** by the produce manager.
- The helping verbs are:
      am, are, is, was, were, be, being, been
      has, have, had
      do, does, did
      can, could, must, may, might, shall, should, will, would

A. Underline the verb phrase, and circle the helping verb in each sentence below.

1. We (have) begun our spring cleaning.

2. Molly and Anne will rake the leaves on the front lawn.

3. Vincent and April must sweep the driveway.

4. The twins, Dawn and Daniela, will pull the weeds.

5. Christopher and his cousin, Lisa, may prepare lunch for the workers.

6. They should wash their hands first.

7. Sandwiches and fruit salad would make a delicious lunch on a hot day.

8. Our next-door neighbor is working on his lawn, too.

9. He has sprayed his front and back lawns with a fertilizer.

10. Every helper must close the garbage bags tightly.

11. Squirrels, raccoons, and large crows would enjoy our garbage.

12. We might finish the outside work today.

B. Use each verb phrase in a sentence.

1. would come _____

2. should choose _____

3. had bought _____

4. might find _____

5. am writing _____

6. will learn _____

7. could become _____

8. were standing _____

More Helping Verbs

- A verb phrase may have more than one helping verb.

  helping verb   main verb
  ↓   ↓

  EXAMPLES: Bill **should have taken** the bus.
                   My tomato plants **have been growing** very quickly.

- In a question or a sentence containing a word such as <u>not</u> or <u>never</u>, the helping verb might be separated from the main verb.

  EXAMPLES: When **will** you **decide** to fix your bicycle?
  Jason **has** not **fixed** his bicycle.

A. Underline the verb phrases, and circle the helping verbs in the sentences below.

1. Our final exam (will be) given on May 10.

2. Many students have been studying every night.

3. My friends and I may be forming a study group.

4. The study group members should be reviewing each chapter.

5. Are you joining our study group?

6. May we meet in your house one afternoon next week?

7. Kim and Tim should have known the answers to the first ten questions.

8. Where have you been all day?

9. I have been looking everywhere for you.

10. I would have met you earlier.

11. The airplane flight has been delayed in Chicago.

12. Would you prefer an earlier flight?

13. No, I had been enjoying a long visit with my grandmother.

14. My parents have been waiting for over two hours in the airport.

15. Lois and Jeanine had been at the pool all day.

16. Will any other friends be swimming in the pool?

17. Several neighborhood children must have been splashing each other.

18. Could Jessica and I take diving lessons next summer?

B. Use each verb phrase in a statement.

1. should have bought _____

2. had been finished _____

C. Use each verb phrase in a question.

1. will be going _____

2. have been practicing _____

Name _____ Date _____

Using *Is/Are* and *Was/Were*

> ■ Use is with a singular subject.
>   EXAMPLE: Tasha **is** the winner.
> ■ Use are with a plural subject.
>   EXAMPLE: The boys **are** walking home.
> ■ Always use are with the pronoun you.
>   EXAMPLE: You **are** absolutely right!

A. Underline the correct verb to complete each sentence.

1. (Is, Are) this tool ready to be cleaned?
2. They (is, are) making peanut brittle.
3. Bill (is, are) the chairperson this week.
4. Where (is, are) my gloves?
5. This tomato (is, are) too ripe.
6. Ryan, (is, are) these your books?
7. Daniel, (is, are) the sandwiches ready?
8. (Is, Are) you going to sing your solo this morning?
9. This newspaper (is, are) the early edition.
10. Carol asked if you (is, are) still coming to the game.

> ■ Use was with a singular subject to tell about the past.
>   EXAMPLE: I **was** there yesterday.
> ■ Use were with a plural subject to tell about the past.
>   EXAMPLE: Kevin and Ray **were** not home.
> ■ Always use were with the pronoun you.
>   EXAMPLE: You **were** only a few minutes late.

B. Underline the correct verb to complete each sentence.

1. Amy and Crystal (was, were) disappointed because they could not go.
2. Our seats (was, were) near the stage.
3. Taro, Bill, and Luis (was, were) assigned to the first team.
4. These pencils (was, were) made by a company in Chicago.
5. There (was, were) only one carton of milk in the refrigerator.
6. Who (was, were) that person on the corner?
7. She (was, were) at my house this morning.
8. You (was, were) the best swimmer in the contest.
9. Those tomatoes (was, were) delicious!
10. He (was, were) late for work today.

Unit 3, Grammar and Usage
© Steck-Vaughn Publishing Company

49

Language Practice 6, SV 7162-7

Verb Tenses

> ■ The **tense** of a verb tells the time of the action or being.
> ■ **Present tense** tells that something is happening now.
>   EXAMPLES: Amanda **dances** in the show. My art lessons **start** today.
> ■ **Past tense** tells that something happened in the past. The action is over.
>   EXAMPLES: Amanda **danced** in the show.
>   My art lessons **started** last June.
> ■ **Future tense** tells that something will happen in the future. Use will
>   with the verb.
>   EXAMPLES: Amanda **will dance** in the show.
>   My art lessons **will start** next month.

A. Underline the verb or verb phrase in each sentence. Then write present, past, or future for the tense of each verb.

1. My neighbor works four days a week.   _____

2. Sometimes I care for her children, Karen and Billy.   _____

3. They play in front of my house.   _____

4. One day Karen threw the ball very hard to Billy.   _____

5. The ball sailed over Billy's head and into the street. _____

6. Billy ran toward the street.   _____

7. I shouted to Billy.   _____

8. Usually, Billy listens to me.   _____

9. I got the ball from the street.   _____

10. Billy's mom called for him to come home.   _____

11. He went as fast as possible.   _____

12. Next time they will play only in the backyard.   _____

B. Rewrite each sentence, changing the underlined verb to the past tense.

1. My little sister will follow me everywhere.

   _____

2. She comes to my friend's house.

   _____

3. She rides my bicycle on the grass.

   _____

Name _____   Date _____

Principal Parts of Verbs

- A verb has four principal parts: **present, present participle, past,** and **past participle.**
- For **regular verbs,** the present participle is formed by adding -ing to the present. It is used with a form of the helping verb be.
- The past and past participles are formed by adding -ed to the present. The past participle uses a form of the helping verb have.

EXAMPLES:

Present	Present Participle	Past	Past Participle
walk	(is) walking	walked	(have, has, had) walked
point	(is) pointing	pointed	(have, has, had) pointed
cook	(is) cooking	cooked	(have, has, had) cooked

- **Irregular verbs** form their past and past participles in other ways. A dictionary shows the principal parts of these verbs.

- Write the present participle, past, and past participle for each verb.

PRESENT	PRESENT PARTICIPLE	PAST	PAST PARTICIPLE
1. walk	(is) walking	walked	(have, has, had) walked
2. visit			
3. watch			
4. follow			
5. jump			
6. talk			
7. add			
8. learn			
9. paint			
10. plant			
11. work			
12. divide			
13. miss			
14. score			
15. call			
16. collect			

Past Tenses of *See, Do,* and *Come*

> ■ Never use a helping verb with: <u>saw</u>   <u>did</u>   <u>came</u>
> ■ Always use a helping verb with: <u>seen</u>   <u>done</u>   <u>come</u>

■ **Underline the correct verb form to complete each sentence.**

1. We (saw, seen) the movie.

2. Suddenly, the whole idea (came, come) to me.

3. Tammy and John (did, done) not do the ironing this morning.

4. They (saw, seen) that a lot of work had to be done to the camp.

5. Who (did, done) the framing of these prints?

6. The rain (came, come) down in sheets.

7. I haven't (did, done) all the errands for Anna.

8. I have (came, come) to help arrange the stage.

9. We have (saw, seen) many miles of beautiful prairie flowers.

10. What have you (did, done) with the kittens?

11. My uncle (came, come) to help me move.

12. I have not (saw, seen) the new apartment today.

13. Why haven't your brothers (came, come) to help us?

14. Haven't you ever (saw, seen) a spider spinning a web?

15. When Lynne and I (came, come) in, we found a surprise.

16. I (saw, seen) the owner about the job.

17. We saw what you (did, done)!

18. Has the mail (came, come) yet?

19. The prettiest place we (saw, seen) was the Grand Canyon.

20. Hasn't Kyle (did, done) a nice job of painting the room?

21. Mr. Jones (came, come) to repair the stove.

22. My dog, Max, (did, done) that trick twice.

23. Josh hadn't (came, come) to the soccer game.

24. Rebecca (saw, seen) the doctor yesterday.

25. Scott has (came, come) to the picnic.

26. Who has (saw, seen) the Rocky Mountains?

27. Deb (did, done) the decorations for the party.

28. She (came, come) to the party an hour early.

29. The bird (saw, seen) the cat near the tree.

30. The painter has (did, done) a nice job on the house.

Name _____ Date _____

Past Tenses of *Eat* and *Drink*

- Never use a helping verb with: <u>ate</u>   <u>drank</u>
- Always use a helping verb with: <u>eaten</u>   <u>drunk</u>

A. Underline the correct verb form to complete each sentence.

1. Have the worms (ate, eaten) the leaves on that tree?

2. We (drank, drunk) the spring water from the mountains.

3. You (ate, eaten) more for breakfast than I did.

4. Haven't you (drank, drunk) a glass of this refreshing lemonade?

5. The hungry hikers (ate, eaten) quickly.

6. Yes, I (drank, drunk) two glasses of lemonade.

7. Have you (ate, eaten) your lunch so soon?

8. Maggie, why haven't you (drank, drunk) your tea?

9. I (ate, eaten) two delicious hamburgers for lunch.

10. We watched the birds as they (drank, drunk) from the birdbath.

11. We (ate, eaten) supper early.

12. Who (drank, drunk) a glass of tomato juice?

13. Have you ever (ate, eaten) a pink grapefruit?

14. Elizabeth, have you (drank, drunk) an extra glass of milk?

15. Have you (ate, eaten) your breakfast yet?

16. Yes, I (drank, drunk) it about noon.

B. Write the correct past tense form of each verb in parentheses to complete each sentence.

1. (eat) Maria had _____ turkey and stuffing at Thanksgiving.

2. (drink) She _____ cranberry juice for breakfast.

3. (eat) Carlos _____ a second sandwich.

4. (drink) At the picnic we had _____ a gallon of lemonade.

5. (drink) Yes, I _____ it at about noon.

6. (eat) Cory hasn't _____ since breakfast.

7. (drink) Father _____ a glass of iced tea.

8. (eat) Did you know that those apples had been _____?

9. (drink) Haven't Mike and Lisa _____ the fresh orange juice?

10. (eat) The people on the train _____ in the dining car.

Past Tenses of *Sing* and *Ring*

> - Never use a helping verb with: <u>sang</u>   <u>rang</u>
> - Always use a helping verb with: <u>sung</u>   <u>rung</u>

A. Underline the correct verb form to complete each sentence.

1. I have never (sang, sung) in public before.

2. Have the church bells (rang, rung)?

3. The group (sang, sung) all their college songs for us.

4. The bell had not (rang, rung) at five o'clock.

5. The children (sang, sung) three patriotic songs.

6. We (rang, rung) their doorbell several times.

7. Which of the three sisters (sang, sung) in the talent show?

8. Who (rang, rung) the outside bell?

9. Patti, have you ever (sang, sung) for the choir director?

10. I (rang, rung) the large old bell that is beside the door.

11. Has she ever (sang, sung) this duet?

12. The Liberty Bell hasn't (rang, rung) in many years.

13. The group (sang, sung) as they had never (sang, sung) before.

14. The ship's bell hasn't (rang, rung).

15. The Canadian singer often (sang, sung) that song.

16. Have you (rang, rung) the bell on that post?

B. Write the correct past tense form of the verb in parentheses to complete each sentence.

1. (ring)   It was so noisy that we couldn't tell if the bell had _____.

2. (sing)   Maria _____ a solo.

3. (sing)   She had never _____ alone before.

4. (ring)   The bells _____ to announce their marriage yesterday.

5. (ring)   Have you _____ the bell yet?

6. (sing)   Who _____ the first song?

7. (ring)   The group _____ bells to play a tune.

8. (sing)   Hasn't she _____ before royalty?

9. (ring)   The boxer jumped up as the bell _____.

10. (sing)   That young boy _____ a solo.

Past Tenses of *Freeze, Choose, Speak,* and *Break*

> ■ Never use a helping verb with: <u>froze</u> <u>chose</u> <u>spoke</u> <u>broke</u>
> ■ Always use a helping verb with: <u>frozen</u> <u>chosen</u> <u>spoken</u> <u>broken</u>

A. Underline the correct verb form to complete each sentence.

1. Haven't those candidates (spoke, spoken) yet?
2. Has the dessert (froze, frozen) in the molds?
3. I (broke, broken) the handle of the hammer.
4. Have you (spoke, spoken) to your friends about the meeting?
5. Hadn't the coach (chose, chosen) the best players today?
6. The dog has (broke, broken) the toy.
7. Has Anna (spoke, spoken) to you about going with us?
8. We (froze, frozen) the ice for our picnic.
9. I believe you (chose, chosen) the right clothes.
10. Dave, haven't you (broke, broken) your bat?
11. Mr. Mann (spoke, spoken) first.
12. Anthony (froze, frozen) the fruit salad for our picnic.
13. You didn't tell me he had (broke, broken) his arm.
14. The men on the team (chose, chosen) their plays carefully.
15. Ms. Ramirez (spoke, spoken) first.
16. Has the river (froze, frozen) yet?

B. Write the correct past tense form of the verb in parentheses to complete each sentence.

1. (freeze) We could not tell if the ice had _____ overnight.
2. (break) The chain on Ann's bicycle had _____ while she rode.
3. (choose) Carol had _____ to be in the play.
4. (speak) No one _____ while the band played.
5. (choose) Tom has _____ to take both tests today.
6. (choose) Jim _____ not to take the test early.
7. (break) No one knew who had _____ the window.
8. (speak) Carol _____ her lines loudly and clearly.
9. (freeze) It was so cold that everything had _____.
10. (speak) The librarian wanted to know who had _____ so loudly.

Name _____   Date _____

Past Tenses of *Know, Grow,* and *Throw*

- Never use a helping verb with: <u>knew</u>   <u>grew</u>   <u>threw</u>
- Always use a helping verb with: <u>known</u>   <u>grown</u>   <u>thrown</u>

A. Underline the correct verb form to complete each sentence.

1. We have (knew, known) her family for years.

2. Weeds (grew, grown) along the park paths.

3. Hasn't Julia (threw, thrown) the softball?

4. I have never (knew, known) a more courageous person.

5. Katie's plants have (grew, grown) very rapidly.

6. How many times have you (threw, thrown) at the target?

7. Has Jonathan (grew, grown) any unusual plants this year?

8. I (knew, known) every person at the meeting.

9. I wish that my hair hadn't (grew, grown) so much this year.

10. Brian, how long have you (knew, known) Lee?

11. The pitcher has (threw, thrown) three strikes in a row.

12. I don't know why the plants (grew, grown) so fast.

13. We (threw, thrown) out many old boxes.

14. Mr. Low has (grew, grown) vegetables this summer.

15. Marty (knew, known) the correct answer.

16. The guard (threw, thrown) the ball to the center.

17. She is the nicest person I have ever (knew, known).

18. The sun (grew, grown) brighter in the afternoon.

B. Write one original sentence with <u>knew</u>. Then write one sentence with <u>known</u>.

1. _____

2. _____

C. Write one original sentence with <u>grew</u>. Then write one sentence with <u>grown</u>.

1. _____

2. _____

D. Write one original sentence with <u>threw</u>. Then write one sentence with <u>thrown</u>.

1. _____

2. _____

Past Tenses of *Blow* and *Fly*

- Never use a helping verb with: <u>blew</u>   <u>flew</u>
- Always use a helping verb with: <u>blown</u>   <u>flown</u>

A. **Underline the correct verb form to complete each sentence.**

1. Flags (flew, flown) from many houses on the Fourth of July.

2. The train whistles have (blew, blown) at every crossing.

3. The birds haven't (flew, flown) south for the winter.

4. The wind (blew, blown) the kites to pieces.

5. The candles (blew, blown) out too soon.

6. Has your friend (flew, flown) her new kite?

7. Yes, she (flew, flown) it this morning.

8. All the papers have (blew, blown) across the floor.

9. Four people (flew, flown) their model airplanes in the tournament.

10. The wind has (blew, blown) like this for an hour.

11. I didn't know that you had (flew, flown) here in a jet.

12. Hasn't the train whistle (blew, blown) yet?

13. The airplanes (flew, flown) in an aviation show.

14. Our largest maple tree had (blew, blown) down last night.

15. The striped hot-air balloon has (flew, flown) the farthest.

16. The judge (blew, blown) the whistle as the runner crossed the finish line.

17. The Carsons have (flew, flown) to Europe.

18. An erupting volcano (blew, blown) the mountain apart.

19. The geese (flew, flown) in formation.

20. The curtains have (blew, blown) open from the breeze.

21. The movie star (flew, flown) in a private jet.

22. A tornado (blew, blown) the roof off a house.

23. A pair of ducks has (flew, flown) overhead.

B. **Write one original sentence with <u>blew</u>. Then write one sentence with <u>blown</u>.**

1. _____

2. _____

C. **Write one original sentence with <u>flew</u>. Then write one sentence with <u>flown</u>.**

1. _____

2. _____

Past Tenses of *Take* and *Write*

- Never use a helping verb with: <u>took</u> <u>wrote</u>
- Always use a helping verb with: <u>taken</u> <u>written</u>

A. Underline the correct verb form to complete each sentence.

1. They (took, taken) the first plane to Tampa.

2. Who has (wrote, written) the best script for the play?

3. Mike hadn't (took, taken) these pictures last summer.

4. Who (wrote, written) the minutes of our last meeting?

5. We (took, taken) down our paintings.

6. Marguerite Henry has (wrote, written) many stories about horses.

7. I (took, taken) my watch to the jeweler for repair.

8. I (wrote, written) for a video catalog.

9. Haven't you (took, taken) your medicine yet?

10. Diana, have you (wrote, written) to your friend?

11. Carlos (took, taken) too much time getting ready.

12. Diane hadn't (wrote, written) these exercises with a pen.

13. Who (took, taken) my magazine?

14. Mario (wrote, written) an excellent business letter.

B. Write the correct past tense form of the verb in parentheses to complete each sentence.

1. (write) Who _____ this short theme?

2. (take) It has _____ me a long time to make this planter.

3. (write) Eve Merriam had _____ this poem.

4. (take) The children have _____ off their muddy shoes.

5. (write) We _____ letters to our state senators.

6. (take) Louisa, have you _____ your dog for a walk?

7. (write) My cousin _____ me a letter about his new house.

8. (write) Robert Frost _____ David's favorite poem.

9. (take) Willie and Sharon _____ the bus to the park.

10. (write) Mr. Bustos _____ an excellent article for our newspaper.

11. (take) The nurse _____ my temperature.

Past Tenses of *Give* and *Go*

■ Never use a helping verb with: <u>gave</u> <u>went</u>
■ Always use a helping verb with: <u>given</u> <u>gone</u>

A. Underline the correct verb form to complete each sentence.

1. Ms. Morris has (gave, given) that land to the city.

2. Where has Ann (went, gone) this afternoon?

3. Carlos (gave, given) a speech on collecting rare coins.

4. My friends (went, gone) to the park an hour ago.

5. Mary, who (gave, given) you this ruby ring?

6. Rob and Carter have (went, gone) to paint the house.

7. Mr. Edwards (gave, given) us ten minutes to take the test.

8. Elaine has (went, gone) to help Eileen find the place.

9. My friends (gave, given) clothing to the people whose house burned.

10. Hasn't Jan (went, gone) to the store yet?

11. The sportscaster has just (gave, given) the latest baseball scores.

12. Charlie (went, gone) to apply for the job.

13. Have you (gave, given) Fluffy her food?

14. Has Miss Martinson (went, gone) to Springfield?

15. I have (gave, given) my horn to my cousin.

16. Paula has (went, gone) to sleep already.

B. Write the correct past tense form of the verb in parentheses to complete each sentence.

1. (go) Paula _____ to sleep already.

2. (give) Has Mrs. Tate _____ the checks to the other employees?

3. (go) Every person had _____ before you arrived.

4. (give) My neighbor was _____ a ticket for speeding.

5. (go) Haven't the Yamadas _____ to Japan for a month?

6. (give) Ms. O'Malley has _____ me a notebook.

7. (go) Haven't you ever _____ to an aquarium?

8. (give) I _____ her my new address.

9. (go) Michael _____ to camp for a week.

10. (give) Ms. Rosen has _____ me driving lessons.

Possessive Pronouns

- A **possessive pronoun** is a pronoun that shows ownership of something.
- The possessive pronouns hers, mine, ours, theirs, and yours stand alone.
  - EXAMPLES: The coat is **mine.** The shoes are **yours.**
- The possessive pronouns her, its, my, our, their, and your must be used before nouns.
  - EXAMPLES: **Her** car is red. **Our** car is black.
- The pronoun his may be used either way.
  - EXAMPLES: That is **his** dog. The dog is **his.**

- **Underline the possessive pronoun in each sentence.**

1. Lora lost her bracelet.

2. David broke his arm.

3. The dogs wagged their tails.

4. The referee blew her whistle.

5. The students should take their books.

6. Musician Louis Armstrong was famous for his smile.

7. Brad entered his sculpture in the contest.

8. I wanted to read that book, but a number of its pages are missing.

9. My aunt and uncle have sold their Arizona ranch.

10. The Inuit build their igloos out of snow blocks.

11. How did Florida get its name?

12. David showed the group his wonderful stamp collection.

13. Coffee found its way from Arabia to Java.

14. The magpie builds its nest very carefully.

15. Pam sprained her ankle while skiing.

16. Lisa drove her car to the top of the peak.

17. Frank left his raincoat in the doctor's office.

18. Isn't Alaska noted for its salmon?

19. Travis brought his mother a beautiful shawl from India.

20. Gina, where is your brother?

21. Manuel forgot about his appointment with the dentist.

22. Joel and Andrew have gone to their swimming lesson.

23. Sandra showed her report to the boss.

24. Juan gave his father a beautiful paperweight.

25. Mr. Owens found his keys.

26. The children broke their swing.

Name _____   Date _____

Indefinite Pronouns

- An **indefinite pronoun** is a pronoun that does not refer to a specific person or thing.
  - EXAMPLES: **Someone** is coming to speak to the group.
  - Does **anyone** know what time it is?
  - **Everybody** is looking forward to the trip.
- Some indefinite pronouns are negative.
  - EXAMPLES: **Nobody** has a ticket.
  - **No one** was waiting at the bus stop.
- The indefinite pronouns anybody, anyone, anything, each, everyone, everybody, everything, nobody, no one, nothing, somebody, someone, and something are singular. They take singular verbs.
  - EXAMPLE: **Everyone is** ready.
- The indefinite pronouns both, few, many, several, and some are plural. They take plural verbs.
  - EXAMPLE: **Several** of us **are** ready.

A. Underline the indefinite pronoun in each sentence below.

1. Everyone helped complete the project.
2. Is somebody waiting for you?
3. Anything is possible.
4. Something arrived in the mail.
5. Everybody looked tired at practice.
6. No one was willing to work longer.
7. Does anyone have a dollar?
8. Both of us were tired.
9. Nothing was dry yet.
10. Does anybody want to go swimming?
11. Someone should speak up.
12. Everybody is hungry now.
13. Each of the cats was black.
14. Some of the dogs bark all the time.
15. Several were empty.
16. No one remembered to bring it.
17. Everyone started to feel nervous.
18. Nobody admitted to being afraid.
19. Everything will be explained.
20. Is anything missing?

B. Complete each sentence with an indefinite pronoun.

1. I can't believe that _____ in my desk has disappeared.

2. Is _____ coming to teach you to run the computer?

3. Every person in class attended today. _____ was absent.

4. She tried to call, but _____ answered the phone.

5. Does _____ remember the address?

6. There is _____ here to see you.

7. Would _____ like a piece of cake?

8. The party was so much fun. _____ enjoyed it.

Subject Pronouns

- A **subject pronoun** is used as the subject or as part of the subject of a sentence.
- The subject pronouns are <u>I</u>, <u>you</u>, <u>he</u>, <u>she</u>, <u>it</u>, <u>we</u>, and <u>they</u>.
    EXAMPLE: **It** has beautiful wings.
- When the pronoun <u>I</u> is used with nouns or other pronouns, it is always named last.
    EXAMPLE: Marie and **I** caught a butterfly.

- **Underline the correct pronoun.**

  1. Carolyn and (I, me) helped repair the car.

  2. (She, Her) is going to the studio.

  3. Why can't Leigh and (I, me) go with them?

  4. (She, Her) and Charles skated all afternoon.

  5. Jaclyn and (I, me) are going to Chicago tomorrow.

  6. (He, Him) played tennis this morning.

  7. Beth and (he, him) were five minutes late yesterday morning.

  8. (She, Her) and (I, me) spent an hour in the library.

  9. Joanne and (I, me) worked until nine o'clock.

  10. (He, Him) and Yuri are going over there now.

  11. May (we, us) carry your packages?

  12. (They, Them) and I are buying some groceries.

  13. Sarah and (I, me) are going with her to the park.

  14. (It, Them) wagged its tail.

  15. (She, You) have a beautiful singing voice, Claire.

  16. (He, Him) is the owner of the suitcase.

  17. Crystal and (I, me) are on the same team.

  18. (She, Her) has started a book club.

  19. (We, Us) are planning a bike trip.

  20. (They, Them) are going to see a Shakespearean play.

  21. Is (she, her) your favorite singer?

  22. Martin and (I, me) would be happy to help you.

  23. (We, Us) work at the post office.

  24. Juan and (we, us) are painting the front porch.

  25. (He, Him) excels as a photographer.

  26. (She, Her) has known us for several years.

  27. (I, Me) am the director of the community choir.

Object Pronouns

- An **object pronoun** is used after an action verb or a preposition, such as <u>after</u>, <u>against</u>, <u>at</u>, <u>between</u>, <u>except</u>, <u>for</u>, <u>from</u>, <u>in</u>, <u>of</u>, <u>to</u>, and <u>with</u>.
- The object pronouns are <u>me</u>, <u>you</u>, <u>him</u>, <u>her</u>, <u>it</u>, <u>us</u>, and <u>them</u>.
  EXAMPLE: The gift was for **him**.
- When the pronoun <u>me</u> is used with nouns or other pronouns, it is always last.
  EXAMPLE: The books were for Kay and **me**.

■ **Underline the correct pronoun.**

1. Tony, are you going with Stephanie and (I, me) to see Rosa?

2. Scott invited Patrick and (I, me) to a movie.

3. I am going to see Mary and (she, her) about this problem.

4. The woman told (us, we) to come for her old magazines.

5. I went with Jan and (she, her) to the hobby show.

6. That dinner was prepared by (them, they).

7. James asked Andrew and (I, me) to the soccer game.

8. Emily and Bev congratulated (he, him).

9. Sharon praised (him, he) for his work.

10. Will you talk to (she, her) about the trip?

11. Ben, can you go with Renee and (I, me)?

12. Pam lectured (us, we) about being on time.

13. The package was leaning against (it, we).

14. They brought the problem to (we, us).

15. It was too hard for (they, them) to solve.

16. Richard gave (I, me) his old goalie's equipment.

17. Anthony is teaching (we, us) Morse code.

18. Please inform (he, him) of the change of plans.

19. Brian offered to help (I, me) hang the curtains.

20. That car belongs to (he, him).

21. Carl didn't see (they, them).

22. Nancy asked him to take a picture of (we, us).

23. Please wait for (she, her) after school.

24. She is in the class with (he, him).

25. Hand the packages to (they, them).

26. Was this really discovered by (she, her)?

27. Would you like to go to dinner with (we, us)?

Name _____ Date _____

Subject Pronouns After Linking Verbs

■ A **linking verb** connects the subject of a sentence with a noun or
adjective that comes after the linking verb.

Subject   Linking Verb   Noun

EXAMPLES: The **baby**   was   **Christopher.**

The **baseball players**   were   **my friends.**

■ Use a subject pronoun after a linking verb.

EXAMPLES: The **baby**   was   **he.**

The **baseball players**   were   **they.**

■ Use a subject pronoun after such phrases as it is or it was.

EXAMPLE: It was **I** who asked the question.

A. Underline the correct pronoun.

1. It was (I, me) who found the keys.
2. It was (she, her) who lost them.
3. The detectives were (we, us).
4. It was (they, them) who looked in the mailbox.
5. The letter carrier is (she, her).
6. It was (he, him) on the telephone.
7. The speakers were Jerald and (I, me).
8. The athlete was (she, her).

9. The photographer was (he, him).
10. That young woman is (she, her).
11. The helper is (he, him).
12. My partners are (they, them).
13. Was it (he, him) who told you?
14. The winner of the race is (she, her).
15. It was (we, us) who were chosen.
16. Was it (I, me) who made the error?

B. Complete these sentences by writing a subject pronoun for the word or words in parentheses.

1. It was _____ who worked out in the gym. (the basketball team)
2. The most talented gymnast is _____. (Susan)
3. Our newest team members are _____. (Jay and Mark)
4. The coach with the whistle is _____. (Laura)
5. The spectators in the gym were _____. (my friends)
6. The one who is on the parallel bars is _____. (Bob)
7. The one who is on the balance beam is _____. (Kristin)
8. Our best vaulter is _____. (Michelle)
9. The athlete on the rings was _____. (Bill)
10. The vice president of the company is _____. (Ms. Walker)

Using *Who/Whom*

- Use <u>who</u> as a subject pronoun.   EXAMPLE: **Who** came to the party?
- Use <u>whom</u> as an object pronoun.   EXAMPLE: **Whom** did the nurse help?
- By rearranging the sentence <u>The nurse did help **whom**?</u>, you can see that <u>whom</u> follows the verb and is the object of the verb. It can also be the object of a preposition.   EXAMPLE: To **whom** did you wish to speak?

- **Complete each sentence with <u>Who</u> or <u>Whom</u>.**

1. _____Who_____ is that man?

2. _____ made the first moon landing?

3. _____ would you choose as the winner?

4. _____ is your best friend?

5. _____ gets the reward?

6. _____ will be staying with you this summer?

7. _____ did the instructor invite to speak to the class?

8. _____ did you see at the park?

9. _____ will you contact at headquarters?

10. _____ will you write about?

11. _____ is available to baby-sit for me on Saturday?

12. _____ did you drive to the store?

13. _____ would like to travel to Hawaii next summer?

14. _____ raced in the track meet?

15. _____ did they meet at the airport?

16. _____ are your three favorite authors?

17. _____ owns that new blue car?

18. _____ did you help last week?

19. _____ wrote that clever poem?

20. _____ will you ask to help you move?

21. _____ brought that salad?

Using Pronouns

■ **Underline the pronouns in each sentence below.**

1. He went with us to the picnic by the lake.

2. Did you find a magazine in the living room?

3. When are we going to meet at the concert?

4. Are we leaving today?

5. Did you see him?

6. She saw them at the party.

7. He spoke to James and me.

8. Who brought the music for you to play?

9. Kristin and I invited them to go to a movie.

10. Mary brought me these pictures she took.

11. Why can't they go with us?

12. I went with her to get the application form.

13. Louis brought you and him some French coins.

14. Between you and me, I think that last program was silly.

15. Did Dorothy explain the experiment to her and him?

16. Did she find them?

17. May I go with you?

18. He and I sat on the benches.

19. They saw me this morning.

20. Who has a library book?

21. For whom shall I ask?

22. I do not have it with me.

23. She told me about the trip to Canada.

24. They are coming to see us.

25. We haven't heard from James since he left.

26. Come with us.

27. Aren't you and I going with Alan?

28. You should plan the theme before you write it.

29. Aren't they coming for us?

30. Kelly and I gave them a new book of stamps.

31. Steve told us an interesting story about a dog.

32. Who is planning a summer vacation?

33. She and I never expected to see you here!

34. We will visit them this evening.

More Pronouns

■ **Underline the correct pronoun.**

1. It was (I, me).

2. Bill and (he, him) are on their way to catch the plane.

3. Nicole and (I, me) have always been good friends.

4. The guard showed (they, them) the entrance to the building.

5. The boss told (I, me) to clean the office.

6. Please take (I, me) to lunch.

7. I am going to wait for (she, her).

8. (Who, Whom) planted those beautiful flowers?

9. Next Saturday Zachary and (I, me) are going fishing.

10. Marie came to see (us, we).

11. To (who, whom) did you send the postcard?

12. This is a secret between you and (I, me).

13. Kevin asked Carolyn to move (us, our) table.

14. The committee asked Michael, Kip, and (I, me) to help serve.

15. Did Ellen bring (she, her)?

16. Jamie told (us, we) to get to the station on time.

17. Grant and (she, her) drove the tractors.

18. (Who, Whom) bought this magazine?

19. The boss brought Matt and Kevin (them, their) checks.

20. Martin took Armando and (I, me) to work this morning.

21. With (who, whom) did you play soccer?

22. Michelle painted (she, her) kitchen yesterday.

23. Seven of (us, we) were named to the board of directors.

24. He completed all of (his, him) math problems this morning.

25. (Us, We) are going to play basketball.

26. She called for Janice and (I, me).

27. (Who, Whom) washed the windows?

28. Joyce and (I, me) will fix the broken latch.

29. We came to see (them, they).

30. Will Pamela or (I, me) go with Jason to (him, his) ranch?

31. For (who, whom) are you looking?

32. Did you know it was (her, she)?

33. Lisa and (her, she) are painting the chairs.

34. (We, Us) are going to the museum on Saturday.

Adjectives

- An **adjective** is a word that describes a noun or a pronoun.
  EXAMPLE: The sky is spotted with **white** clouds.
- Adjectives usually tell **what kind, which one,** or **how many.**
  EXAMPLES: **white** roses, **that** mitt, **fifteen** cents

A. Choose an appropriate adjective from the box to describe each noun.

brave	foolish	gorgeous	hasty	shiny
cold	fragrant	happy	polite	sly

1. _____ scout

2. _____ flower

3. _____ worker

4. _____ water

5. _____ fox

6. _____ girls

7. _____ sunset

8. _____ dimes

9. _____ prank

10. _____ deeds

B. Write three adjectives that could be used to describe each noun.

1. flowers _____   _____   _____

2. an automobile _____   _____   _____

3. a friend _____   _____   _____

4. a bicycle _____   _____   _____

5. snow _____   _____   _____

6. a baby _____   _____   _____

7. a sunrise _____   _____   _____

8. a book _____   _____   _____

9. a kitten _____   _____   _____

10. a train _____   _____   _____

11. a mountain _____   _____   _____

12. the wind _____   _____   _____

13. a river _____   _____   _____

14. a house _____   _____   _____

Name _____   Date _____

> - The **articles** a, an, and the are called **limiting adjectives**.
> - Use a before words beginning with a consonant sound.
>   EXAMPLES: **a** bugle, **a** mountain, **a** sail
> - Use an before words beginning with a vowel sound.
>   EXAMPLES: **an** oboe, **an** island, **an** anchor

C. Write a or an in each blank.

1. _____ salesperson

2. _____ train

3. _____ newspaper

4. _____ iceberg

5. _____ friend

6. _____ election

7. _____ welder

8. _____ piano

9. _____ game

10. _____ ant

11. _____ eye

12. _____ army

13. _____ telephone

14. _____ orange

15. _____ country

16. _____ airplane

17. _____ oak

18. _____ engine

19. _____ ear

20. _____ state

21. _____ elm

22. _____ shoe

23. _____ object

24. _____ basket

25. _____ apple

26. _____ ounce

27. _____ error

28. _____ tablet

29. _____ desk

30. _____ holiday

31. _____ accident

32. _____ astronaut

33. _____ box

34. _____ fire

35. _____ pilot

36. _____ mechanic

37. _____ entrance

38. _____ evergreen

39. _____ aviator

40. _____ hundred

41. _____ picture

42. _____ elephant

43. _____ letter

44. _____ umbrella

45. _____ announcer

46. _____ onion

47. _____ umpire

48. _____ car

49. _____ ice cube

50. _____ elevator

Name _____ Date _____

Proper Adjectives

■ A **proper adjective** is an adjective that is formed from a proper noun.
It always begins with a capital letter.

EXAMPLES: **Proper Noun**   **Proper Adjective**
Poland   Polish
Germany   German
Paris   Parisian

A. Write a proper adjective formed from each proper noun below. You may wish to check the spelling in a dictionary.

1. South America _____
2. Africa _____
3. England _____
4. Mexico _____
5. France _____
6. Russia _____
7. America _____
8. Rome _____
9. Alaska _____

10. Canada _____
11. Norway _____
12. Scotland _____
13. Ireland _____
14. China _____
15. Spain _____
16. Italy _____
17. Hawaii _____
18. Japan _____

B. Write sentences using proper adjectives you formed in Exercise A.

1. ___Many South American countries have warm climates._____
2. _____
3. _____
4. _____
5. _____
6. _____
7. _____
8. _____
9. _____
10. _____

Name _____   Date _____

Demonstrative Adjectives

- A **demonstrative adjective** is an adjective that points out a specific person or thing.
- This and that describe singular nouns. This points to a person or thing nearby, and that points to a person or thing farther away.
  EXAMPLES: **This** room is my favorite. **That** man is running very fast.
- These and those describe plural nouns. These points to persons or things nearby, and those points to persons or things farther away.
  EXAMPLES: **These** women are the best players. **Those** houses need painting.
- The word them is a pronoun. Never use it to describe a noun.

A. Underline the correct demonstrative adjective.

1. Please hand me (those, this) red candles.

2. Where did you buy (these, that) large pecans?

3. Did you grow (these, them) roses in your garden?

4. Please bring me (those, that) wrench.

5. Where did Marc find (these, this) watermelon?

6. (Those, Them) glasses belong to Mike.

7. Do you want one of (these, this) calendars?

8. May I use one of (these, them) pencils?

9. Did you see (those, them) films of Africa?

10. Calvin, where are (those, that) people going?

11. Did you see (those, them) police officers?

12. Please put (those, this) books in the box.

13. (That, Those) floor needs to be cleaned.

14. Sarah and Joe might buy (those, that) car.

15. (That, These) cabinets will be repainted.

16. Please close (that, those) door.

17. Will you fix the flat tire on (this, these) bike?

18. (This, Those) letter needs a stamp before you mail it.

B. Write four sentences using this, that, these, or those.

1. _____

2. _____

3. _____

4. _____

Comparing with Adjectives

- An adjective has three degrees of comparison: **positive, comparative,** and **superlative.**
- The simple form of the adjective is called the **positive** degree.
    - EXAMPLE: Anita is **tall.**
- When two people or things are being compared, the **comparative** degree is used.
    - EXAMPLE: Anita is **taller** than Nancy.
- When three or more people or things are being compared, the **superlative** degree is used.
    - EXAMPLE: Anita is the **tallest** person in the group.
- For all adjectives of one syllable and a few adjectives of two syllables, add -er to form the comparative degree and -est to form the superlative degree.
    - EXAMPLE: rich — richer — richest
- If the adjective ends in -y, change the -y to -i and add -er or -est.
    - EXAMPLE: tiny — tinier — tiniest

- **Write the comparative and superlative forms.**

	POSITIVE	COMPARATIVE	SUPERLATIVE
1.	smooth		
2.	young		
3.	sweet		
4.	strong		
5.	lazy		
6.	great		
7.	kind		
8.	calm		
9.	rough		
10.	narrow		
11.	deep		
12.	short		
13.	happy		
14.	cold		
15.	pretty		

Name _____   Date _____

More Comparing with Adjectives

■ For some adjectives of two syllables and all adjectives of three or more syllables, use <u>more</u> to form the comparative and <u>most</u> to form the superlative.
   EXAMPLES: He thinks that the lily is **more** fragrant than the tulip.
   He thinks that the carnation is the **most** fragrant flower of all.
■ Comparison of adjectives also can be used to indicate less or least of a quality. Use <u>less</u> to form the comparative and <u>least</u> to form the superlative.
   EXAMPLES: I see Jo **less** often than I see Terry.
   I see Josh **least** often of all.
■ Some adjectives have irregular comparisons.
   EXAMPLES: good, better, best   bad, worse, worst

A. Write the comparative and superlative forms using <u>more</u> and <u>most</u>.

POSITIVE	COMPARATIVE	SUPERLATIVE
1. energetic		
2. courteous		
3. impatient		
4. important		
5. difficult		
6. wonderful		
7. gracious		
8. agreeable		

B. Write the comparative and superlative forms using <u>less</u> and <u>least</u>.

POSITIVE	COMPARATIVE	SUPERLATIVE
1. helpful		
2. friendly		
3. serious		
4. agreeable		
5. faithful		
6. comfortable		
7. patient		
8. reliable		

Name _____   Date _____

C. Write the correct degree of comparison for the adjective in parentheses.

1. (near)   Which planet is _____ the earth, Venus or Jupiter?

2. (tall)   Who is the _____ of the three people?

3. (helpful)   Who is _____, Sandra or Linda?

4. (young)   Who is _____, Jack or Tim?

5. (difficult)   I think this is the _____ problem in the lesson.

6. (good)   Is "A Ghost Story" a _____ story than "The Last Leaf"?

7. (small)   What is our _____ state?

8. (hot)   In our region, August is usually the _____ month.

9. (young)   Hans is the _____ person at the factory.

10. (wide)   The Amazon is the _____ river in the world.

11. (old)   Who is _____, David or Steve?

12. (large)   What is the _____ city in your state?

13. (courteous)   Dan is always the _____ person at a party.

14. (good)   This poem is the _____ one I have read this year.

15. (cold)   This must be the _____ night so far this winter.

16. (studious)   Of the two sisters, Andrea is the _____.

17. (tall)   Who is _____, Kay or Carol?

18. (wealthy)   This is the home of the _____ banker in our city.

19. (fast)   Who is the _____ worker in the office?

20. (useful)   Which is _____, electric lights or the telephone?

21. (beautiful)   Your garden is the _____ one I have seen.

22. (narrow)   That is the _____ of all the bridges on the road.

23. (large)   Cleveland is _____ than Cincinnati.

24. (good)   Of the three books, this one is the _____.

25. (bad)   That is the _____ collection in the museum.

26. (famous)   Washington became the _____ general of the Revolution.

27. (beautiful)   I think tulips are the _____ kind of flower.

Adverbs

- An **adverb** is a word that describes a verb, an adjective, or another adverb.
  EXAMPLES: The parade moved **slowly**. Your tie is **very** colorful.
  You did this **too** quickly.
- An adverb usually tells **how, when, where,** or **how often.**
- Many adverbs end in -ly.

A. Write two adverbs that could be used to describe each verb.

1. laugh _____

2. talk _____

3. stand _____

4. sing _____

5. swim _____

6. eat _____

7. read _____

8. work _____

9. write _____

10. walk _____

11. jump _____

12. move _____

13. run _____

14. speak _____

15. listen _____

16. drive _____

17. sit _____

18. dance _____

B. Use each adverb in a sentence.

well	regularly	early
softly	very	here

1. _____

2. _____

3. _____

4. _____

5. _____

6. _____

Name _____ Date _____

C. Underline the adverb or adverbs in each sentence.

1. The old car moved slowly up the hill.

2. She answered him very quickly.

3. We arrived at the party too early, so we helped with the decorations.

4. The family waited patiently to hear about the newborn baby.

5. Cindy drove the car very cautiously in the snowstorm.

6. Does Marshall always sit here, or may I have this seat?

7. They walked very rapidly in order to get home before the rainstorm.

8. The dog ran swiftly toward its home.

9. Emily quietly waited her turn while others went ahead.

10. These oaks grow very slowly, but they are worth the long wait.

11. May I speak now, or should I wait for his call?

12. We searched everywhere for the inflatable rafts and life preservers.

13. The nights have been extremely warm, so we go swimming every evening.

14. He always speaks distinctly and practices good manners.

15. Can you swim far underwater without coming up for air?

16. Come here, and I'll show you ladybugs in the grass.

17. Please answer quickly so that we can finish before five o'clock.

18. Deer run very fast, especially at the first sign of danger.

19. I suddenly remembered that I left my jacket in the park.

20. The snow fell softly on the rooftops of the mountain village.

21. I can pack our lunches and be there by noon.

22. She wrote too rapidly and made a mistake.

23. Winters there are extremely cold, but summers are very pleasant.

24. The pianist bowed politely to the audience.

25. You are reading too rapidly to learn something from it.

26. The team played extremely well.

27. The cat walked softly toward a fly on the windowpane.

28. Everyone listened carefully to the sound of a bluebird singing.

29. We walked wearily toward the bus in the hot sun.

30. We crossed the street very carefully at the beginning of the parade.

31. We eagerly watched the game from the rooftop deck of our building.

32. The recreation center was finished recently.

33. We walked everywhere yesterday.

34. My friend dearly loves her red hat.

35. I have read this book before.

36. He wants badly to learn to play the guitar.

Comparing with Adverbs

> - An **adverb** has three degrees of comparison: **positive, comparative,** and **superlative.**
> - The simple form of the adverb is called the **positive** degree.
>   EXAMPLE: Joe worked **hard** to complete the job.
> - When two actions are being compared, the **comparative** degree is used.
>   EXAMPLE: Joe worked **harder** than Jim.
> - When three or more actions are being compared, the **superlative** degree is used.
>   EXAMPLE: Tony worked **hardest** of all.
> - Use -er to form the comparative degree and use -est to form the superlative degree of one-syllable adverbs.
> - Use more or most with longer adverbs and with adverbs that end in -ly.
>   EXAMPLE: Jan danced **more** gracefully than Tania.
>   Vicki danced the **most** gracefully of all.

- **Complete each sentence using the comparative or superlative form of the underlined adverb.**

1. David can jump <u>high</u>. Diane can jump _____ than David.

   Donna can jump the _____ of all.

2. Grant arrives <u>late</u> for the party. Gina arrives _____

   than Grant. Gail arrives _____ of anyone.

3. Dawn walks <u>slowly</u> in the park. Tomás walks _____

   than Dawn. Sam walks _____ of all.

4. Jean spoke <u>clearly</u> before the class. Jon spoke _____

   than Jean. Joseph spoke _____ of all the students.

5. Alex scrubbed <u>hard</u>. Anne scrubbed _____ than Alex.

   Alice scrubbed the _____ of all.

6. You can lose weight <u>quickly</u> by running. A nutritious diet works _____

   than just running. Of all weight-loss programs, combining the two works

   _____.

7. Tania played the flute <u>beautifully</u>. Tara played the clarinet even _____.

   Rick played the oboe the _____ of them all.

8. Chris has been waiting <u>long</u>. Mr. Norris has been waiting even _____.

   Justin has been waiting the _____ of all.

Using *Doesn't* and *Don't*

- *Doesn't* is the contraction of <u>does not</u>. Use it with singular nouns and the pronouns <u>he</u>, <u>she</u>, and <u>it</u>.
    EXAMPLES: The dog **doesn't** want to play. She **doesn't** want to go.
- *Don't* is the contraction of <u>do not</u>. Use it with plural nouns and the pronouns <u>I</u>, <u>you</u>, <u>we</u>, and <u>they</u>.
    EXAMPLES: The children **don't** have their books. We **don't** have time.

- **Underline the correct contraction to complete each sentence.**

1. I (doesn't, don't) know why he (doesn't, don't) like that movie star.

2. Why (doesn't, don't) the caretaker open the gates earlier?

3. (Doesn't, Don't) your sister coach the team, Tom?

4. (Doesn't, Don't) this office need more fresh air?

5. (Doesn't, Don't) this sweater belong to you, Katie?

6. We (doesn't, don't) go home at noon for lunch.

7. (Doesn't, Don't) your friend attend the state university?

8. Terry (doesn't, don't) want to miss the parade.

9. Angelo (doesn't, don't) like to play tennis.

10. It (doesn't, don't) take long to learn to swim.

11. Some of the elevators (doesn't, don't) go to the top floor.

12. Eric (doesn't, don't) know how to drive a car.

13. He (doesn't, don't) know that we are here.

14. We (doesn't, don't) listen to our radio often.

15. Why (doesn't, don't) Craig get here on time?

16. This problem (doesn't, don't) seem difficult to me.

17. (Doesn't, Don't) it look hot outside?

18. Why (doesn't, don't) Paul go, too?

19. She (doesn't, don't) want to go to the movie.

20. Kelly (doesn't, don't) have that written in her notebook.

21. (Doesn't, Don't) you want to go with us?

22. Why (doesn't, don't) your friend come to our meetings?

23. Neil (doesn't, don't) go to night school.

24. Melissa (doesn't, don't) eat ice cream.

25. Jody and Ray (doesn't, don't) like science fiction movies.

26. The people (doesn't, don't) have to wait outside.

27. (Doesn't, Don't) you want to come with us?

28. They (doesn't, don't) know if it will rain today.

Using *May/Can* and *Teach/Learn*

- Use <u>may</u> to ask for permission.
  EXAMPLE: **May** I go with you?
- Use <u>can</u> to express the ability to do something.
  EXAMPLE: James **can** swim well.

A. Complete each sentence with <u>may</u> or <u>can</u>.

1. Adam, _____ you whistle?

2. His dog _____ do three difficult tricks.

3. Miss Nance, _____ I leave work early?

4. I _____ see the airplane in the distance.

5. Chris, _____ you tie a good knot?

6. Carlos, _____ I drive your car?

7. You _____ see the mountains from here.

8. My friend _____ drive us home.

9. The Garcias _____ speak three languages.

10. _____ I examine those new books?

- <u>Teach</u> means "to give instruction."
  EXAMPLE: I'll **teach** you how to shoot free throws.
- <u>Learn</u> means "to acquire knowledge."
  EXAMPLE: When did you **learn** to speak Spanish?

B. Complete each sentence with <u>teach</u> or <u>learn</u>.

1. I think he will _____ me quickly.

2. I will _____ to recite that poem.

3. Did Jamie _____ you to build a fire?

4. The women are going to _____ to use the new machines.

5. Will you _____ me to play tennis?

6. My brother is going to _____ Billy to skate.

7. Would you like to _____ the rules of the game to them?

8. No one can _____ you if you do not try to _____.

Using *Sit/Set* and *Lie/Lay*

> ■ Sit means "to take a resting position." Its principal parts are sit, sitting, and sat.
>   EXAMPLES: Please **sit** here. He **sat** beside her.
> ■ Set means "to place." Its principal parts are set, setting, and set.
>   EXAMPLES: Will you please **set** this dish on the table?
>   She **set** the table for dinner last night.

A. Underline the correct verb.

1. Please (sit, set) down, Kathleen.

2. Where should we (sit, set) the television?

3. Where do you (sit, set)?

4. Pamela, please (sit, set) those plants out this afternoon.

5. (Sit, Set) the basket of groceries on the patio.

6. José usually (sits, sets) on this side of the table.

7. Please come and (sit, set) your books down on that desk.

8. Have you ever (sat, set) by this window?

9. Does he (sit, set) in this seat?

10. Why don't you (sit, set) over here?

> ■ Lie means "to recline" or "to occupy a certain space." Its principal parts are lie, lying, lay, and lain.
>   EXAMPLES: Why don't you **lie** down for a while?
>   He **has lain** in the hammock all afternoon.
> ■ Lay means "to place." Its principal parts are lay, laying, and laid.
>   EXAMPLES: The men **are laying** new carpeting in the house.
>   Who **laid** the wet towel on the table?

B. Underline the correct verb.

1. Where did you (lie, lay) your gloves, Beth?

2. (Lie, Lay) down, Spot.

3. He always (lies, lays) down to rest when he is very tired.

4. Where have you (lain, laid) the evening paper?

5. Please (lie, lay) this box on the desk.

6. Do not (lie, lay) on that dusty hay.

7. (Lay, Lie) the papers on top of the desk.

8. I (laid, lain) the shovel on that pile of dirt.

9. I need to (lie, lay) down to rest.

10. She has (laid, lain) on the sofa all morning.

Prepositions

- A **preposition** is a word that shows the relationship of a noun or a pronoun to another word in the sentence.
  EXAMPLES: Put the package **on** the table. Place the package **in** the desk.
- These are some commonly used prepositions:

about	against	at	between	from	of	through	under
above	among	behind	by	in	on	to	upon
across	around	beside	for	into	over	toward	with

- **Draw a line under each preposition or prepositions in the sentences below.**

1. The grin on Juan's face was bright and warm.

2. He greeted his cousin from Brazil with a smile and a handshake.

3. They walked through the airport and toward the baggage area.

4. Juan found his bags between two boxes.

5. The two cousins had not seen each other for five years.

6. They could spend hours talking about everything.

7. Juan and Luis got into Juan's truck.

8. Juan drove Luis to Juan's family's ranch.

9. It was a long ride across many hills and fields.

10. Luis rested his head against the seat.

11. Soon they drove over a hill and into a valley.

12. The ranch was located across the Harrison River.

13. The house stood among a group of oak trees.

14. Juan parked the truck beside the driveway.

15. They walked across the driveway and toward the house.

16. Juan's mother, Anita, stood behind the screen door.

17. Juan's family gathered around Luis.

18. Everyone sat on the porch and drank lemonade.

19. "Tell us about our relatives in Brazil," Rosa asked.

20. "You have over twenty cousins in my area," said Luis.

21. They go to school, just like you do.

22. Then everyone went into the house and ate dinner.

23. Juan's family passed the food across the table.

24. "Many of these dishes come from old family recipes," he said.

25. "It is wonderful to be among so many relatives," Luis said.

26. After dinner, everyone went to the living room.

27. Luis showed them photographs of his home in Brazil.

Name _____ Date _____

Prepositional Phrases

> ■ A **prepositional phrase** is a group of words that begins with a preposition and ends with a noun or pronoun. EXAMPLE: Count the books **on the shelf.**
> ■ The noun or pronoun in a prepositional phrase is called the **object of the preposition.** EXAMPLE: Count the books on the **shelf.**

■ **Put parentheses around each prepositional phrase. Then underline each preposition, and circle the object of the preposition.**

1. The founders (of the United States) had a vision (of a great country).
2. We climbed into the station wagon.
3. Many stars can be seen on a clear night.
4. The top of my desk has been varnished.
5. Have you ever gone through a tunnel?
6. Place these memos on the bulletin board.
7. We have a display of posters in the showcase in the corridor.
8. Carol, take these reports to Ms. Garza.
9. What is the capital of Alabama?
10. The fabric on this antique sofa came from France.
11. Are you a collector of minerals?
12. I am going to Julia's house.
13. The hillside was dotted with beautiful wild flowers.
14. The rain beat against the windowpanes.
15. We placed a horseshoe above the door.
16. This poem was written by my oldest sister.
17. Great clusters of grapes hung from the vine.
18. Is he going to the race?
19. A herd of goats grazed on the hillside.
20. Are you carrying those books to the storeroom?
21. Our car stalled on the bridge.
22. My family lives in St. Louis.
23. A small vase of flowers was placed in the center of the table.
24. The group sat around the fireplace.
25. The cold wind blew from the north.
26. Doris hit the ball over the fence.
27. The dog played with the bone.
28. High weeds grow by the narrow path.

Prepositional Phrases as Adjectives/Adverbs

> ■ A prepositional phrase can be used to describe a noun or a pronoun. Then the prepositional phrase is being used as an **adjective** to tell which one, what kind, or how many.
>   EXAMPLE: The chair **in the corner** needs to be repaired.
>   The prepositional phrase in the corner tells **which** chair.
> ■ A prepositional phrase can be used to describe a verb. Then the prepositional phrase is being used as an **adverb** to tell how, where, or when.
>   EXAMPLE: Mrs. Porter repaired the chair **during the evening.**
>   The prepositional phrase during the evening tells **when** Mrs. Porter repaired the chair.

■ **Underline the prepositional phrase in each sentence. Write <u>adjective</u> or <u>adverb</u> to tell how the phrase is used.**

1. Sue went to the library. _____

2. She needed a book about gardening. _____

3. The shelves in the library contained many books. _____

4. She asked the librarian with blue shoes. _____

5. The librarian in the green dress was very helpful. _____

6. She taught Sue about the card catalog. _____

7. The card catalog has a card for every book. _____

8. The cards are organized in alphabetical order. _____

9. Some gardening books were in the health section. _____

10. Sue's trip to the library was a great success. _____

11. She took several books with her. _____

12. Sue read them at home. _____

13. The window seat in the living room was her favorite spot. _____

14. Sue looked out the window. _____

15. Her own garden by the backyard fence was dead. _____

16. The vegetables from last year's garden had been delicious. _____

17. She would plant more vegetables near the house. _____

18. Then she would have many vegetables in the summer. _____

Name _____   Date _____

Conjunctions

- A **conjunction** is a word used to join words or groups of words.
  - EXAMPLES: Sally **and** Barb worked late. We worked **until** he arrived.
- These are some commonly used conjunctions:

although	because	however	or	that	until	whether
and	but	if	since	though	when	while
as	for	nor	than	unless	whereas	yet

- Some conjunctions are used in pairs. These include either . . . or, neither . . . nor, and not only . . . but also.

A. Underline each conjunction in the sentences below.

1. We waited until the mechanic replaced the part.

2. Plums and peaches are my favorite fruits.

3. The wind blew, and the rain fell.

4. Please call Alan or Grant for me.

5. A conjunction may connect words or groups of words.

6. Cotton and wheat are grown on nearby farms.

7. Neither Ann nor Bonnie is my cousin.

8. Their home is not large, but it is comfortable.

9. Ron and Sue arrived on time.

10. Do not move the vase, for you may drop it.

B. Complete each sentence with a conjunction.

1. I cannot leave _____ the baby-sitter arrives.

2. We must hurry, _____ we'll be late for work.

3. Battles were fought on the sea, on the land, _____ in the air.

4. Charles _____ Rick went to the movie, _____ Donald did not.

5. Please wait _____ Elizabeth gets ready.

6. Juan _____ I will carry that box upstairs.

7. Peter _____ Dan are twins.

8. We will stay home _____ you cannot go.

9. This nation exports cotton _____ wheat.

10. _____ the children _____ the parents liked the violent movie.

Name _____   Date _____

Interjections

- An **interjection** is a word or group of words that expresses emotion.
  EXAMPLE: **Hurrah!** Our team has won the game.
- If the interjection is used to express sudden or strong feeling, it is followed by an exclamation mark.
  EXAMPLE: **Wow!** You've really done it this time.
- If the interjection is used to express mild emotion, it is followed by a comma.
  EXAMPLE: **Oh,** I see what you mean.
- These are some commonly used interjections:

ah	good grief	oh	ugh
aha	great	oops	well
alas	hurrah	sh	whew

- **Write sentences with the following interjections.**

1. Ah _____

2. Wow _____

3. Oh _____

4. Ugh _____

5. Ouch _____

6. Oops _____

7. Hurrah _____

8. Oh no _____

9. Hey _____

10. Sh _____

11. Help _____

12. Well _____

13. Whew _____

14. Oh my _____

15. Hush _____

16. Hooray _____

17. Aha _____

18. Ha _____

Name _____   Date _____

Unit 3 Test

Choose which kind of noun is underlined in each sentence.

1. Our <u>vacation</u> was wonderful.   **A** ○ common   **B** ○ proper   **C** ○ possessive

2. The judge told <u>Mr. Clark</u> he was free to go.   **A** ○ common   **B** ○ proper   **C** ○ possessive

3. My <u>brother's</u> ranch is in Wyoming.   **A** ○ common   **B** ○ proper   **C** ○ possessive

Choose the correct form of the noun.

4. singular   **A** ○ men   **B** ○ man   **C** ○ men's

5. possessive   **A** ○ brush   **B** ○ brush's   **C** ○ brushes

6. plural   **A** ○ horse   **B** ○ horses   **C** ○ horse's

Choose each sentence with an appositive.

7. **A** ○ James, please bake my favorite dessert.

   B ○ He told Eric, his brother, to be careful.

   C ○ Did you borrow my hat, Sharon?

   D ○ Hoover Dam took years to build.

8. **A** ○ Don't tell my secret, please.

   B ○ Finally, she remembered his name.

   C ○ No amount of time will ease the pain.

   D ○ The nurse, a young man, saved her life.

Choose the correct verb(s) to complete each sentence.

9. I ___ waiting here for an hour.   **A** ○ been   **B** ○ had   **C** ○ have been

10. Did Kurt tell you that these ___ his photographs?   **A** ○ was   **B** ○ is   **C** ○ are

11. He ___ work at the library this year.   **A** ○ don't   **B** ○ doesn't   **C** ○ doing

12. ___ I have your new phone number?   **A** ○ May   **B** ○ Does   **C** ○ Can

13. Can you ___ me how to play the guitar?   **A** ○ learn   **B** ○ learned   **C** ○ teach

14. Will Joan have time to ___ down before lunch?   **A** ○ lie   **B** ○ set   **C** ○ lay

15. She ___ speak if there is time.   **A** ○ may   **B** ○ was   **C** ○ is

16. Please ___ the book on the table.   **A** ○ lie   **B** ○ set   **C** ○ sit

17. He said he ___ want any meat.   **A** ○ don't   **B** ○ doesn't   **C** ○ do

18. It takes time to ___ something new.   **A** ○ learn   **B** ○ teach   **C** ○ taught

19. ___ Carol going to pick up her package?   **A** ○ Are   **B** ○ Were   **C** ○ Is

20. I am going to ___ down now.   **A** ○ lie   **B** ○ lay   **C** ○ lying

21. She wants to ___ how to ski.   **A** ○ teach   **B** ○ learned   **C** ○ learn

22. Jason ___ need anything from the store.   **A** ○ do   **B** ○ doesn't   **C** ○ don't

Choose the correct past tense verb to complete each sentence.

23. Several of us ___ in a play.   **A** ○ had sang   **B** ○ sung   **C** ○ have sung

24. I ___ my favorite vase yesterday.   **A** ○ broke   **B** ○ had broke   **C** ○ broken

25. We ___ to the park for lunch.   **A** ○ gone   **B** ○ went   **C** ○ have went

26. The bottle of soda ___ .   **A** ○ freezed   **B** ○ frozed   **C** ○ froze

27. She ___ out her old clothes.   **A** ○ throw   **B** ○ thrown   **C** ○ threw

28. Who ___ this story?   **A** ○ wrote   **B** ○ write   **C** ○ written

29. Sylvia ___ her a present.   **A** ○ gived   **B** ○ gave   **C** ○ given

Choose the correct adjective or adverb to complete each sentence.

30. This is the ___ ice cream I've ever had.   **A** ○ smoother   **B** ○ smoothest   **C** ○ most smooth

31. A squirrel can run ___ than a dog.   **A** ○ quickest   **B** ○ quickly   **C** ○ more quickly

Choose the correct pronoun to complete each sentence.

32. Have you ever met ___ parents?   **A** ○ hers   **B** ○ their   **C** ○ them

33. ___ was waiting for me when I got home.   **A** ○ They   **B** ○ Both   **C** ○ No one

34. ___ and Laurel are going to the concert tonight.   **A** ○ He   **B** ○ Him   **C** ○ Her

35. Please tell ___ to meet us at six o'clock.   **A** ○ them   **B** ○ their   **C** ○ they

36. Chuck gave the prettiest flower to ___ .   **A** ○ she   **B** ○ hers   **C** ○ her

37. It was ___ who cooked the turkey.   **A** ○ her   **B** ○ we   **C** ○ us

38. Nina chose ___ as her partner?   **A** ○ whom   **B** ○ she   **C** ○ who

Choose the correct word to go with the article.

39. a   **A** ○ house   **B** ○ onion   **C** ○ umbrella

40. an   **A** ○ tornado   **B** ○ boat   **C** ○ icicle

Choose whether each underlined group of words is (A) a prepositional phrase used as an adjective, (B) a prepositional phrase used as an adverb, or (C) not a prepositional phrase.

41. I learned about outdoor safety <u>at a seminar</u>.   **A** ○   **B** ○   **C** ○

42. We all liked our instructor <u>from England</u>.   **A** ○   **B** ○   **C** ○

43. She was <u>very knowledgeable</u> about safety.   **A** ○   **B** ○   **C** ○

Using Capital Letters

> ■ **Capitalize** the first word of a sentence.
>   EXAMPLE: Let's take a walk to the park.
> ■ Capitalize the first word of a quotation.
>   EXAMPLE: Joseph said, "It's time for lunch."

A. Circle each letter that should be capitalized. Write the capital letter above it.

1. haven't you made an appointment to meet them?

2. the teenagers will go to the game together.

3. danielle asked, "how did she like the book?"

4. the family moved to another state last year.

5. "bring your scripts to the practice," said the director.

6. who wrote this article for the newspaper?

7. the woman said, "my party is in one week."

8. "have some more carrot sticks," said the host.

> ■ Capitalize the first word of every line of poetry.
>   EXAMPLE: The strong winds whipped
>   The sails of the ship
> ■ Capitalize the first, last, and all important words in the titles of books, poems, songs, and stories.
>   EXAMPLES: *Gone with the Wind*   "America the Beautiful"

B. Circle each letter that should be capitalized. Write the capital letter above it.

1. i eat my peas with honey;

   i've done it all my life.

   it makes the peas taste funny,

   but it keeps them on the knife!

2. it's midnight, and the setting sun

   is slowly rising in the west;

   the rapid rivers slowly run,

   the frog is on his downy nest.

3. Who wrote the poem "the children's hour"?

4. My favorite novel is *a wrinkle in time.*

5. The high school band played "stand by me."

6. During the summer, Kim read *adam of the road.*

7. Carla gave her poem the title "chasing the wind."

- Capitalize all **proper nouns.**
  EXAMPLES: Sarah, Dad, Arbor Street, England, Maine, Arctic Ocean,
  Ural Mountains, Columbus Day, February, Academy School, *Ocean Queen*
- Capitalize all **proper adjectives.** A proper adjective is an adjective that
  is made from a proper noun.
  EXAMPLES: the Spanish language, American food, Chinese people

---

C. Rewrite the following paragraph. Be sure to add capital letters where they are needed.

chris and her friends went to a festival in chicago, illinois. Some of them
tasted greek pastry and canadian cheese soup. charley thought that the italian
sausage and mexican tacos were delicious! laurel tried an unusual japanese
salad. They all watched some irish folk dancers and listened to german music.

_____

_____

_____

_____

_____

_____

_____

_____

D. Circle each letter that should be capitalized. Write the capital letter above it.

1. Did anita and her family drive through arizona, new mexico, and colorado?

2. Isn't brazil larger in area than the united states?

3. Did mark twain live in the small town of hannibal, missouri?

4. Have you read the story of martin luther king?

5. I have been reading about the solomon islands.

6. The north sea is connected with the english channel by the strait of dover.

7. At thirteen, sam houston moved to tennessee from lexington, virginia.

8. Isn't st. augustine the oldest city in the united states?

9. Is nairobi the capital of kenya?

10. Our friend brought japanese money back from her trip.

> ■ Capitalize a person's title when it comes before a name.
>   EXAMPLES: Doctor Baker, Governor Alvarez, Senator Washington
> ■ Capitalize abbreviations of titles.
>   EXAMPLES: Dr. Garcia, Supt. Barbara Shurna, Mr. J. Howell, Sr.

E. Circle each letter that should be capitalized. Write the capital letter above it.

1. Did captain cheng congratulate sergeant walters on his promotion?

2. The new health plan was developed by dr. ruth banks and mr. juan gomez.

3. After an introduction, pres. alice slater presented the next speaker, mr. allen norman.

4. When did principal grissom invite mayor hadley to attend the graduation ceremony?

5. Officer halpern was the first to stand up when judge patterson entered the courtroom.

6. How long has mrs. frank been working for president howell?

7. Does prof. mary schneider teach this course, or does dr. david towne?

8. Prince andrew of england will tour the southern states in the fall.

9. Senator alan howell is the uncle of supt. joyce randall.

> ■ Capitalize abbreviations of days and months, parts of addresses, and
>   titles of members of the armed forces. Also capitalize all letters in
>   abbreviations for states.
>   EXAMPLES: Fri., Jan., 3720 E. Franklin Ave., Gen. H. J. Farrimond,
>   Los Angeles, CA, Dallas, TX

F. Circle each letter that should be capitalized. Write the capital letter above it.

1. capt. margaret k. hansen

   2075 lakeview st.

   phoenix, az 85072

2. jackson school Track Meet

   at wilson stadium

   tues., sept. 26, 10:30

   649 n. clark blvd.

3. mr. jonathan bernt

   150 telson rd.

   markham, ontario L3R 1E5

4. lt. gary l. louis

   5931 congress rd.

   syracuse, ny 13217

5. thanksgiving Concert

   wed., nov. 23, 11:00

   Practice tues., nov. 22, 3:30

   See ms. evans for details.

6. gen. david grimes

   329 n. hayes st.

   louisville, ky 40227

Using End Punctuation

> ■ Use a **period** at the end of a declarative sentence.
>   EXAMPLE: Theresa's aunt lives in Florida.
> ■ Use a **question mark** at the end of an interrogative sentence.
>   EXAMPLE: Will you carry this package for me?

A. Use a period or question mark to end each sentence below.

1. Ms. Clark has moved her law office____

2. Isn't this Dorothy's baseball glove____

3. Are you moving to Massachusetts next month____

4. It's too late to buy tickets for the game____

5. Our program will begin in five minutes____

6. Does your sister drive a truck____

7. Ms. Tobin's store was damaged by the flood____

8. Are you going to Rebecca's party____

9. Lucy did not take the plane to St. Petersburg____

10. Do you have a stamp for this envelope____

11. Have you ever seen Clarence laugh so hard____

12. President Sophia Harris called the meeting to order____

13. Will Gilmore Plumbing be open on Labor Day____

14. School ends the second week in June____

15. We are going camping in Canada this summer____

B. Add the correct end punctuation where needed in the paragraph below.

Have you ever been to the Olympic Games____ If not, have you ever seen them on television____ I hope to see them in person some day____ The Olympic Games are held every four years in a different country____ The games started in ancient Greece, but the games as we now know them date back to 1896____ Some of the finest athletes in the world compete for bronze, silver, and gold medals____ Can you think of a famous Olympic athlete____ What is your favorite Olympic sport____ It could be a winter or summer sport because the games are held for each season____ One American athlete won seven gold medals in swimming____ Can you imagine how excited that athlete must have felt, knowing that he had represented America so well____ That is the American record to date____ However, there will be plenty more chances for that record to be broken____

Name _____   Date _____

> - Use a period at the end of an imperative sentence.
>   EXAMPLE: Close the door to the attic.
> - Use an **exclamation point** at the end of an exclamatory sentence and after an interjection that shows strong feelings.
>   EXAMPLES: What a great shot! I'd love to go with you! Wow!

C. Add periods and exclamation points where needed in the sentences below.

1. Address the envelope to Dr. George K. Zimmerman____

2. How nicely dressed you are____

3. Hurry____ The bus is ready to leave____

4. Get some paints for your next art lesson____

5. Shake hands with Mr. D. B. Norton____

6. Oops____ I spilled the glass of orange juice____

7. Carry this bag to the car in the parking lot____

8. What a great view you have from your apartment window____

9. Wipe the counter when you're through eating____

10. Oh, what a beautiful painting____

11. I can't wait until summer vacation____

12. Please take this to the post office for me____

13. Just look at the size of the fish he caught____

14. I've never seen a larger one____

15. Get the net from under the life preserver____

16. I sure hope the pictures come out well____

D. Add the correct end punctuation where needed in the paragraph below.

The state of Maine in New England is a wonderful place to visit in the summer or winter____ Have you ever been there____ It is best known for its rocky coastline on the Atlantic Ocean____ Visitors often drive along the rugged coast____ There are numerous quaint sea towns along the coast that date back to the 1600s____ What a long time ago that was____ Mount Katahdin and the northern part of the Appalachian Mountains are ideal places for winter sports, such as downhill and cross-country skiing____ If you've never seen a deer or moose, you'd probably see plenty of them while hiking in Acadia National Park____ It has over 30,000 acres____ Do you know anything about Maine's local fish____ Well, there are many kinds that are native to its rivers and lakes____ But Maine is famous for its Atlantic lobsters____ Rockport and Rockland are two of the largest cities for lobster fishing____ Lobsters from northern Maine are flown all over the world____ Blueberries are another big product of Maine____ Have you ever had wild blueberries____ Some people consider them to be the best____

Name _____ Date _____

Using Commas

> ■ Use a **comma** between words or groups of words in a series.
>   EXAMPLE: Be sure your business letter is brief, courteous, and correct.
> ■ Use a comma before a conjunction in a compound sentence.
>   EXAMPLE: Neal sketched the cartoon, and Clare wrote the caption.

A. Add commas where needed in the sentences below.

1. The United States exports cotton corn and wheat to many countries.

2. The children played softball ran races and pitched horseshoes.

3. Lauren held the nail and Tasha hit it with a hammer.

4. Alice Henry Carmen and James go to the library often.

5. The pitcher threw a fastball and the batter struck out.

6. Sara peeled the peaches and Victor sliced them.

7. The mountains were covered with forests of pine cedar and oak.

8. Craig should stop running or he will be out of breath.

9. Baseball is Lee's favorite sport but Sue's favorite is football.

10. Limestone marble granite and slate are found in Vermont New Hampshire and Maine.

11. The rain fell steadily and the lightning flashed.

12. Mindy enjoyed the corn but Frank preferred the string beans.

> ■ Use a comma to set off a quotation from the rest of a sentence.
>   EXAMPLES: "We must get up early," said Mom.
>   Mom said, "We must get up early."

B. Add commas before or after the quotations below.

1. "Please show me how this machine works" said Carolyn.

2. "Be sure you keep your eyes on the road" said the driving instructor.

3. Rick replied "I can't believe my ears."

4. Gail said "Travel is dangerous on the icy roads."

5. "Paul studied piano for two years" said Ms. Walters.

6. Alex said "That goat eats everything in sight."

7. "Let's go to the park for a picnic" said Marie.

8. "Wait for me here" said Paul.

9. Tom said "Sandra, thank you for the present."

10. "I'm going to the game with Al" remarked Frank.

11. Al asked "What time should we leave?"

12. Chris remembered "I was only five when we moved to New York."

■ Use a comma to set off the name of a person who is being addressed.
    EXAMPLE: Betty, did you find the answer to your question?
■ Use a comma to set off words like <u>yes</u>, <u>no</u>, <u>well</u>, and <u>oh</u> at the beginning of a sentence.
    EXAMPLE: No, I haven't seen Jack today.
■ Use a comma to set off an appositive.
    EXAMPLE: Jack, Mary's brother, is going to college next fall.

C. Add commas where needed in the sentences below.

1. Miss Hunt do you know the answer to that question?

2. Can't you find the book I brought you last week Roger?

3. Dr. Levin the Smith's dentist sees patients on weekends.

4. Oh I guess it takes about an hour to get to Denver.

5. Joe may Sam and I go to the ball game?

6. Our neighbor Billy Johnson is a carpenter.

7. What is the population of your city Linda?

8. Well I'm not sure of the exact number.

9. Beth are you going skiing this weekend?

10. What time are you going to the concert Greg?

11. Joseph our friend coaches the softball team.

12. Sue have you seen a small black cat around your neighborhood?

13. Jeff do you know Mr. D. B. Norton?

14. No I don't think we've ever met.

15. Sally and John would you like to go shopping on Saturday?

16. Mrs. Porter the principal is retiring this year.

17. Yes the teachers are planning a retirement dinner for her.

18. Mrs. Porter and her husband Hal plan to move to Oregon.

D. Add commas where needed in the paragraph below.

I have two friends who are always there for me and I tell them everything. So it was a surprise to me when Carol my oldest friend said "Well when are you moving?" I said "What do you mean?" She said "I don't believe you our dearest friend wouldn't tell us first what was going on in your life." Margie my other friend said "I feel the same way. Ann why on earth did we have to hear about this from Ray?" "Margie and Carol I don't know what you're talking about" I said. "Oh don't be ashamed" said Margie. "We know you must have some good reason and we're waiting to hear it." "No I don't have any reason because I'm not moving" I said. "Ray that prankster must have been trying to play a joke on us" said Carol.

Using Quotation Marks and Apostrophes

- Use **quotation marks** to show the exact words of a speaker. Use a comma or another punctuation mark to separate the quotation from the rest of the sentence.
  - EXAMPLES: "Do you have a book on helicopters?" asked Tom.
  - James said, "It's right here."
- A quotation may be placed at the beginning or at the end of a sentence. It may also be divided within the sentence.
  - EXAMPLES: Deborah said, "There are sixty active members."
  - "Morton," asked Juanita, "have you read this magazine article?"

A. Add quotation marks and other punctuation where needed in the sentences below.

1. Dan, did you ever play football asked Tim.

2. Morris asked Why didn't you come in for an interview?

3. I have never said Laurie heard a story about a ghost.

4. Selina said Yuri thank you for the present.

5. When do we start on our trip to the mountains asked Stan.

6. Our guest said You don't know how happy I am to be in your house.

7. My sister said Kelly bought those beautiful baskets in Mexico.

8. I'm going to plant the spinach said Doris as soon as I get home.

- Use an **apostrophe** in a contraction to show where a letter or letters have been taken out.
  - EXAMPLES: Amelia **didn't** answer the phone. **I've** found my wallet.
- Use an apostrophe to form a possessive noun. Add -'s to most singular nouns. Add -' to most plural nouns. Add -'s to a few nouns that have irregular plurals.
  - EXAMPLES: A **child's** toy was in our yard. The **girls'** toys were in our yard. The **children's** toys were in our yard.

B. After each sentence below, write the word in which an apostrophe has been left out. Add the apostrophe where needed.

1. Many players uniforms are red. _____

2. That dog played with the babys shoe. _____

3. Julio isnt coming with us to the library. _____

4. Its very warm for a fall day. _____

5. The captains ship was one of the newest. _____

6. Marcia doesnt sing as well as my sister does. _____

7. Mens coats are sold in the new store. _____

Using Colons and Hyphens

> - Use a **colon** after the greeting in a business letter.
>   EXAMPLES: Dear Sir: Dear Ms. Franklin:
> - Use a colon between the hour and the minute when writing time.
>   EXAMPLES: 2:00   7:45   9:37
> - Use a colon to introduce a list.
>   EXAMPLE: The suitcase contained these items: a toothbrush, a brush, a comb, and some clothing.

A. Add colons where needed in the sentences or phrases below.

1. The program begins at 8 3 0.

2. Dear Mrs. Sanchez

3. These are the students who must return library books Julia Turner, Carl Porter, Crystal Fletcher, and Asako Satoshi.

4. Beverly wakes up every morning at 6 1 5.

5. Dear Mr. Graham

> - Use a **hyphen** between the parts of some compound words.
>   EXAMPLES: father-in-law   blue-black   well-known
>   thirty-six   part-time   one-fourth
> - Use a hyphen to separate the syllables of a word that is carried over from one line to the next.
>   EXAMPLE: After eating dinner, we watched a television show about tor-nadoes in the Midwest.

B. Add hyphens where needed in the sentences below.

1. A driving safety expert will visit the school to give a presen tation on seat belts.

2. There should be forty two people at the lecture.

3. I searched high and low, but I couldn't seem to find that new, yellow zip per I bought today.

4. My mother in law is coming from Florida.

5. In fifty eight years of driving, he has a nearly perfect record.

6. Ralph and Victor came late to the meeting, but Lora and Angela arrived ear ly and stayed late.

7. George could lift weights with ease, and Alberto was able to swim twenty one laps without stopping.

8. Our air conditioning unit broke on the hottest day of this summer.

9. Donna had to go inside to change her clothes because Scoot, her frisky pup py, got his muddy paws on her.

Unit 4 Test

Choose the word in each sentence that should be capitalized.

1. I had sweet and sour chicken at a chinese restaurant.

   A ○ sweet   **B** ○ chicken   **C** ○ chinese   **D** ○ restaurant

2. My parents celebrated their wedding anniversary in may.

   A ○ parents   **B** ○ wedding   **C** ○ anniversary   **D** ○ may

3. Who wrote the adventure story *The Call of the wild*?

   A ○ wrote   **B** ○ adventure   **C** ○ story   **D** ○ *wild*

4. I met mayor Bradley at the celebration yesterday.

   A ○ met   **B** ○ mayor   **C** ○ celebration   **D** ○ yesterday

5. She lives at 503 north Bryer Street, on the corner near the store.

   A ○ corner   **B** ○ store   **C** ○ north   **D** ○ near

6. The earthquake shook the ground in Los Angeles, california.

   A ○ california   **B** ○ earthquake   **C** ○ ground   **D** ○ shook

Choose the correct answer to the question.

In which sentences are commas used correctly?

7. **A** ○ I called, but Amy wasn't home.

   B ○ We ate cheese, apples and bread.

   C ○ "No" she said "I, can't go."

   D ○ The answer is, that we just don't know.

8. **A** ○ Stop look, and listen Bob.

   B ○ "We would like to go," said Hans.

   C ○ Enrique, my friend lives, in Houston.

   D ○ My arm hurts but, it's okay.

9. **A** ○ My best friend, Pat and I can come.

   B ○ Tell me now, what you want.

   C ○ Well, yes, I do like spinach.

   D ○ I left and then, Karen went home.

10. **A** ○ Tanya, did you see the show?

   B ○ Becky asked "How are you, Eric?"

   C ○ Well, how will you get there Jay?

   D ○ She told the truth, and was not believed.

Choose the correct answer to the question.

In which sentences is end punctuation used correctly?

11. **A** ○ How wonderful our trip was?

   B ○ I can't remember.

   C ○ Are you going to the fair!

   D ○ I just love this book so much.

12. **A** ○ Wow. That's a great album.

   B ○ Can you go with us!

   C ○ Have you seen a shooting star?

   D ○ What a great ceremony?

13. **A** ○ Take control of the car.

   B ○ Please, will you come!

   C ○ Don't I know you.

   D ○ Let me read that first?

14. **A** ○ That program was awful?

   B ○ Could you hear her sing!

   C ○ Let me watch for them.

   D ○ Ouch. That hurt.

Choose the correct answers to each question.

In which sentences are quotation marks used correctly?

15. **A** ○ "No," said Tom, "I can't go.

   B ○ "Are you leaving?" asked Lee.

   C ○ "Yes, said Joe, I am."

   D ○ Carol said, Be sure to write!"

16. **A** ○ "How are you"? asked Dan

   B ○ "How, asked Sue, do you do it?"

   C ○ "When can you come?" I asked.

   D ○ "Yes! said Marie, "I can."

17. **A** ○ For now, I'll just wait," said Todd.

   B ○ "Why don't you ask? said Luis.

   C ○ "Please let me in!" said Carmen.

   D ○ "No, said Jeff, "I'm not ready yet."

18. **A** ○ Brent said, "Throw that away."

   B ○ "It's still good, said Rebecca."

   C ○ "Now," said Lily, just watch me!"

   D ○ "Don't forget to jump, said Ruth.

Choose the correct answers to each question.

In which sentences or phrases are colons used correctly?

23. **A** ○ Dear Mom:

   B ○ Sincerely yours:

   C ○ 10:30 P.M.

   D ○ 615 A.M.

24. **A** ○ Take these things: a book, a pen, and some paper.

   B ○ Leave the house by 1130, or you'll be late.

   C ○ Don't worry: I'm fine.

   D ○ She called the following: names.

25. **A** ○ Dear Sir:

   B ○ The play begins at 83:0.

   C ○ Please: use this door.

   D ○ Thank you: for all your help.

In which sentences are apostrophes used correctly?

19. **A** ○ I ca'nt meet you until 6:30.

   B ○ Il'l walk the dog.

   C ○ It's 12:00, and I am late!

   D ○ The dog shook it's head.

20. **A** ○ I'm sorry I can't be there.

   B ○ Lets' go together.

   C ○ I need two day's notice.

   D ○ Were all staying home.

21. **A** ○ Tell them the'yre almost here.

   B ○ Our neighbor's party was loud.

   C ○ Two trees' caught on fire.

   D ○ Listen to the'ir reasons.

22. **A** ○ The picture tell's the story.

   B ○ I love Charlotte's home.

   C ○ His cats' were both black.

   D ○ The papers have'nt been delivered.

In which sentences are hyphens used correctly?

26. **A** ○ My father-in-law came to visit.

   B ○ My part time-job is fun.

   C ○ There were more than thirty two-people.

   D ○ One half-of the cake was eaten.

27. **A** ○ Dorothy was fif-teen minutes late.

   B ○ A firefighter gave a presenta-tion on fire safety.

   C ○ Twenty six-pizzas were delivered to the party.

   D ○ That monument is over one-hundred years old.

28. **A** ○ The air conditioner was-broken.

   B ○ She is twenty-one years old.

   C ○ The sun-set was orange red.

   D ○ He likes his sister in-law.

Writing Sentences

> - Every sentence has a base consisting of a simple subject and a simple predicate.
>   EXAMPLE: Dolphins leap.
> - Expand the meaning of a sentence by adding adjectives, adverbs, and prepositional phrases to the sentence base.
>   EXAMPLE: **The sleek** dolphins **suddenly** leap **high into the air.**

A. Expand the meaning of each sentence base by adding adjectives, adverbs, and/or prepositional phrases. Write each expanded sentence.

1. (Dinner cooks.) _____

2. (Clown chuckled.) _____

3. (Car raced.) _____

4. (Dancer spun.) _____

5. (Panthers growled.) _____

6. (Leaves fall.) _____

7. (Bread baked.) _____

8. (Lake glistened.) _____

9. (Ship glides.) _____

B. Write five sentence bases. Then write an expanded sentence containing each sentence base.

1. _____
   _____

2. _____
   _____

3. _____
   _____

4. _____
   _____

5. _____
   _____

Writing Topic Sentences

■ A **topic sentence** is the sentence within a paragraph that states the main idea. It is often placed at the beginning of a paragraph.
EXAMPLE:
   The trip to the national park was a great success. First, the visitors learned a lot from their guide about the park. They learned that the forest was created by people, not by nature. To their surprise, they found out that the park had more than five hundred species of plants. Then they went on a hike and even spotted a falcon flying overhead. Finally, the visitors had a wonderful picnic lunch and headed back home.

A. Write a topic sentence for each paragraph below.

1.   Some jewelry is made out of feathers, leather, shells, or wood. Other jewelry is crafted from gold, silver, brass, copper, or other metals. Gems and unusual stones are added for their beauty and value.

   Topic Sentence: _____

2.   A pet goldfish needs clean water. A pump should be placed in the water to supply fresh air. The water temperature must be constant, and it must not go below 27°C (80°F). The goldfish should be fed flaked fish food or small insects.

   Topic Sentence: _____

3.   When Jana crawls over to a kitchen cabinet, she whips the door open to see what's behind it. With a little help from Jana, the pots and pans are on the floor in no time. If she sees a bag of groceries, Jana has to investigate the contents. After she is tucked in bed for the night, this toddler loves to climb out of her crib and explore.

   Topic Sentence: _____

B. Write a topic sentence for each of the paragraph ideas below.

1. birthday parties _____

2. a great adventure _____

3. a great president _____

4. a favorite holiday _____

5. homework _____

6. video games _____

7. vacations _____

8. the Olympics _____

Writing Supporting Details

> ■ The idea expressed in a topic sentence can be developed with sentences containing **supporting details.** Details can include facts, examples, and reasons.

A. Read the topic sentence below. Then read the sentences that follow. Circle the seven sentences that contain details that support the topic sentence.

Topic Sentence: The Big Dipper Theme Park is a wonderful place to go for a fun-filled day.

1. The roller coaster is the most popular ride in the park.

2. The park was built in 1959.

3. You can test your pitching skills at the game booths.

4. You can win a stuffed animal at one of the pitching games.

5. Young children can enjoy a part of the park made especially for them.

6. We had sandwiches and potato salad for lunch.

7. The train ride is a pleasant way to relax and see the park.

8. However, the water rides are a great way to beat the heat.

9. What do you like to do during summer vacation?

10. The sky ride provides a grand tour of the park from high in the air.

B. Choose one of the topic sentences below. Write it on the first line. Then write five sentences that contain supporting details. The details can be facts, examples, or reasons.

1. Exercise is important for maintaining good health.

2. Being the oldest child in a family has its advantages.

3. The teen-age years are a time of change.

4. True friendship makes life more interesting and fun.

_____

_____

_____

_____

_____

_____

_____

_____

_____

Name _____   Date _____

Topic and Audience

> - The **topic** of a paragraph is the subject of the paragraph.
> - The **title** of a paragraph should be based on the topic.
> - The **audience** is the person or persons who will read the paragraph.
>   EXAMPLES: teachers, classmates, readers of the school newspaper, friends, family members

A. Suppose that you chose the topic <u>watching TV</u>. Underline the sentence that you would choose for the topic sentence.

1. Watching TV is one of the best ways to learn about things.

2. Watching TV is a waste of time.

3. The time children spend watching TV should be limited.

B. Think about the topic sentence you chose in Exercise A. Then underline the audience for whom you would like to write.

1. your friends

2. your family members

3. readers of a newspaper

C. Write a paragraph beginning with the topic sentence you chose in Exercise A. Keep your audience in mind as you write. Be sure to write a title.

_____

_____

_____

_____

_____

_____

_____

_____

_____

_____

_____

_____

_____

Name _____   Date _____

Taking Notes

- **Note-taking** is an important step when writing a report.
- You can find information for reports in encyclopedias, books, and magazines.
- Before you begin, organize your research questions.
- Write information accurately and in your own words.
- Take more notes than you expect to need, so you won't have to go back to your sources a second time.

Portfolio

A. Underline a topic below that interests you.

1. a favorite hobby

2. the stars or planets

3. a historical figure

4. a species of animal

5. movies

6. a favorite sport

7. a favorite food

8. fashion or costumes

9. gardening

10. airplanes

B. Gather some sources of information about your topic. Write the name of your topic on the first line below. For example, if you have chosen "a favorite food," you might write the name of that particular food. Then write notes about the topic on the remaining lines.

_____

_____

_____

_____

_____

_____

_____

_____

_____

_____

_____

_____

_____

_____

_____

_____

Name _____   Date _____

Outlining

- Organize your thoughts before writing by making an **outline.** An outline consists of the title of the topic, **main headings** for the main ideas, and **subheadings** for the supporting ideas.
- Main headings are listed after Roman numerals. Subheadings are listed after capital letters.

Topic: First aid for burns
Main heading   I. Keeping the wound clean
Subheadings {   A. Applying thick, clean dressing
                       B. Avoiding sprays or oils
                    II. Easing pain
                       A. Applying ice packs
                       B. Putting injured area in ice water

- Write an outline for the topic you chose in Exercise A on page 103. Use the sample outline as a guide.

Topic: _____

    I. _____

       A. _____

       B. _____

    II. _____

       A. _____

       B. _____

    III. _____

       A. _____

       B. _____

    IV. _____

       A. _____

       B. _____

    V. _____

       A. _____

       B. _____

Name _____   Date _____

Writing a Report

> ■ A **report** is a series of informative paragraphs covering a main topic.
> Each paragraph has a topic sentence and other sentences that contain
> supporting details. Begin with a paragraph that introduces the report,
> and end with a paragraph that concludes the report.

A. Read the paragraphs below.

Exploring the Mystery Planets: Uranus, Neptune, and Pluto

The planets Uranus, Neptune, and Pluto are difficult to study because of their distance
from Earth. However, scientists are not completely without information about these planets.
They know, for example, that Uranus is more than twice as far from Earth as Saturn is. They
also know that Neptune is half again as far from Earth as Uranus. Both Saturn and Uranus
are four times the size of Earth.

Scientists have explored the mysteries of Uranus. As Uranus orbits the sun every 84
years, it rolls around on its side. Although it is larger than Earth and orbits the sun more
slowly, Uranus spins on its axis very rapidly. It completes a full rotation in 15 hours, 30
minutes. Five known satellites accompany Uranus, along with a system of nine dark rings
that were discovered in 1977. The diameter of Uranus is 32,500 miles (52,200 kilometers),
and the planet lies 1.78 billion miles (2.87 billion kilometers) from the sun. Because of this
great distance, the temperature of Uranus is $-360°F$ ($-220°C$), far too cold for any earth
creature to survive.

Scientists have also explored the mysteries of Neptune. At a distance of 2.8 billion miles
(4.5 billion kilometers) from the sun, Neptune appears through a telescope as a greenish-
blue disc. Neptune is somewhat smaller than Uranus, having a diameter of about 30,000
miles. It is also very cold ($-328°F$, or $-200°C$). Two of Neptune's satellites have been
named Nereid and Triton. In the summer of 1989, *Voyager 2* finally passed Neptune and,
among other things, revealed that there are up to five rings around the planet.

It was 1930 before Pluto, the last planet in our solar system, was discovered. The "new"
planet is 3.67 billion miles (6 billion kilometers) from the sun and takes 248 years to
complete its orbit. In comparison, Earth takes only 365 days to complete a single orbit. While
Pluto has not been measured exactly, scientists believe that it has a diameter of 1,600 miles
(2,670 kilometers).

There are more interesting facts about Pluto. It also has a satellite, called Charon, which is
five times closer to Pluto than our moon is to Earth. The yellowish color of Pluto indicates
that it has very little atmosphere. Pluto's distance from the sun indicates that its climate is
the coldest of the nine planets in our solar system.

Many mysteries remain concerning Uranus, Neptune, and Pluto, despite the fact that so
much has been discovered. The questioning minds of the twenty-first century will continue
our search for the secrets of space.

B. Circle the word or phrase that best completes each statement about this report.

1. Most of the report's supporting details are (facts, examples, reasons).

2. The writer of this report has included the (color, discoverer, diameter) of each of the three planets.

3. The writer does not discuss the relationship of the mystery planets to (Earth, Mars, the sun).

C. Underline the topic sentence in each paragraph.

Revising and Proofreading

- **Revising** gives you a chance to rethink and review what you have written and to improve your writing. Revise by adding words and information, by taking out unneeded words and information, and by moving words, sentences, and paragraphs around.
- **Proofreading** has to do with checking spelling, punctuation, grammar, and capitalization. Use proofreader's marks to show changes needed in your writing.

Proofreader's Marks

≡	⊙	⑤ᵖ
Capitalize.	Add a period.	Correct spelling.
/	∧	¶
Make a small letter.	Add something.	Indent for new paragraph.
∧	⤴	⟶
Add a comma.	Take something out.	Move something.

A. Rewrite the paragraph below. Correct the errors by following the proofreader's marks.

¶ yellowstone national park is the oldest and largest park national in the united states. It is located partly in northwestern wyoming, partly in southern montana, and partley in easturn idaho idaho. during the summur, large parts of park the were damaged by fire. A serious lack of rein was part of the reason the fire was sew severe, one fire threatened almost to destroy the park's famous lodge, which is constructed entirely of wood. fortunately, firefighters' efforts saved the lodge from desturction. today, the forests are slowly recovering from the fires.

_____

_____

_____

_____

_____

_____

_____

_____

B. Read the paragraphs below. Use proofreader's marks to revise and proofread the paragraphs. Then write your revised paragraphs below.

although yellowstons national park is the largest national national park in the United states, other national parks are also well-known yosemite national park in california has acres of Mountain Scenery and miles of hiking trails. Won of the world's largest biggest waterfalls can also be found in yosemite.

mammoth cave national park in kentucky features a huge underground cave the cave over has 212 miles of corridors it also have underground lakes rivers and waterfalls this cave system is estimated to be millions of years old

many pepul are surprized to learn that their are national parks in alaska and hawaii. mount McKinley the highest mountain in north america is located in denali national park in alaska. you can travel to hawaii and visit hawaii volcanoes national park this Park Has too active volcanoes rare plants and animals.

_____
_____
_____
_____
_____
_____
_____
_____
_____
_____
_____
_____
_____
_____

Writing a Business Letter

- ■ A **business letter** has six parts.
  - • The **heading** contains the address of the person writing and the date.
  - • The **inside address** contains the name and address of the person to whom the letter is written.
  - • The **greeting** tells to whom the letter is written. Use "Dear Sir or Madam" if you are unsure who will read the letter. Use a colon after the greeting in a business letter.
  - • The **body** is the message of the letter. It should be brief, courteous, and to the point.
  - • The **closing** is the ending that follows the body.
  - • The **signature** is the name of the person who is writing the letter.
- ■ When writing a business letter, remember the following:
  - • Use business-size paper and envelopes.
  - • Center your letter on the page, leaving at least a one-inch margin on each side.
  - • Include specific information, such as quantities, sizes, numbers, brands, prices, manner of shipment, and amount of payment.
  - • When you have finished, reread your letter. Rewrite it if you are not satisfied with any part of it.

A. Study this business letter. Then answer the questions below.

heading	572 Ironwood Avenue Orlando, FL 32887 April 4, 1994
inside address	Order Department Perfection Computer Company 9940 Main Street Brooklyn, NY 11227

greeting
body
	Dear Sir or Madam:
	   Please send me one copy of Making Friends With Your Computer. Enclosed is $16.95 to cover the cost of the book plus shipping and handling.
	   Thank you for your assistance.

closing **signature**	Sincerely yours, *Chris Morrow* Chris Morrow

1. Who wrote the letter? _____

2. What is the greeting? _____

3. Where is Perfection Computer Company located? _____

_____

4. When was the letter written? _____

> ■ Use a business-size envelope for a business letter. Be sure to include your return address. Check both addresses to be sure they are correct.

Chris Morrow
572 Ironwood Avenue
Orlando, FL 32887

Order Department
Perfection Computer Company
9940 Main Street
Brooklyn, NY 11227

B. **Write a brief business letter asking for information about the Chicago Fire that you can use in a report. Write to the Chicago Historical Society at 1601 North Clark Street in Chicago, Illinois. The zip code is 60616. Then circle the parts of the letter that would appear on the envelope.**

_____

_____

_____

_____

_____

_____

_____

_____

_____

_____

_____

_____

_____

_____

Unit 5 Test

Read the paragraph. Then choose the correct answer to each question.

Did you know that penguins actually prefer to live in very cold climates? In fact, most often they lay their eggs on ice. Fortunately, a penguin has thick layers of fat to help keep it warm. Some male penguins actually have extra rolls of fat, which they use to keep their newborn penguins warm. Originally, penguins were capable of flying, but millions of years ago, their wings developed into flippers which now function as paddles. Perhaps the most interesting thing of all about a penguin is the way it walks. Penguins actually waddle because they have such extremely short legs!

1. Which sentence can best be used as a topic sentence for the paragraph above?

    A ○ Penguins like cold weather.

    B ○ Male penguins care for their young.

    C ○ The penguin is an unusual bird.

    D ○ Penguins lay eggs.

2. Which sentence would be the best supporting detail for the paragraph above?

    A ○ Penguins live in the southern half of the world.

    B ○ Penguins are popular additions to most zoos.

    C ○ All penguins are black and white.

    D ○ The male penguin produces a milky substance in its throat, which it uses to feed its young.

3. Which audience would be the most interested in this paragraph?

    A ○ grandparents   **B** ○ soccer coaches   **C** ○ animal lovers   **D** ○ nurses

Choose the sentence that does not contain details that support the topic sentence.

4. **Topic Sentence:** A chef's job is very demanding.

    A ○ Great chefs can make very good money.

    B ○ Chefs must cook many things at once.

    C ○ They must make sure a party's meals are ready at the same time.

    D ○ Chefs must cook food as quickly as possible.

5. **Topic Sentence:** Wild mustangs are increasing in number.

    A ○ People with ranches are letting mustangs roam free.

    B ○ Wild mustangs are smaller than other breeds.

    C ○ Some people adopt wild mustangs and care for them.

Choose the correct answer to each question.

6. Which is <u>not</u> good advice for taking research notes?

   A ○ Use reference materials for information.

   B ○ Take notes, then organize research questions.

   C ○ Always put information in your own words.

   D ○ Take more notes than you expect to need.

7. Which is <u>not</u> part of an outline?

   A ○ subheadings

   B ○ title

   C ○ main headings

   D ○ topic sentence

8. Which is <u>not</u> part of a report?

   A ○ title

   B ○ main headings

   C ○ topic sentences

   D ○ informative paragraphs

9. Which is <u>not</u> part of a business letter?

   A ○ body

   B ○ heading

   C ○ signature

   D ○ title

10. Which is <u>not</u> part of writing a good business letter?

   A ○ Reread and rewrite, if necessary.

   B ○ Use the person's first name in the greeting.

   C ○ Include specific information.

   D ○ Use business-size paper and envelopes.

11. Which part of a business letter follows the body?

   A ○ greeting

   B ○ heading

   C ○ inside address

   D ○ closing

Choose the correct revision of each underlined sentence.

12. <u>dr. Jones Came, I and Paul visited with him.</u>

   A ○ When Dr. Jones came Paul and I visited with him.

   B ○ When Mr. Jones visited, I and Paul came with him.

   C ○ Dr. Jones came, and Paul and I visited with him.

   D ○ When Dr. Jones came, Paul and I visited with him.

13. <u>tell Kay what that she herd was a the secret.</u>

   A ○ Tell Kay, what she herd was the secret.

   B ○ Tell Kay what she heard that was a secret.

   C ○ Tell Kay that what she heard was a secret.

   D ○ Tell Kay there what she heard.

14. <u>the gold rush, people streamed form over all the country to Californa.</u>

   A ○ All the people from the country streamed to California.

   B ○ During the Gold Rush, people from all over went to California.

   C ○ People streamed from all over the country to the Gold Rush.

   D ○ During the Gold Rush, people from all over the country streamed to California.

Name _____ Date _____

Dictionary: Guide Words

- A **dictionary** is a reference book that contains definitions of words and other information about their history and use.
- **Entries** in a dictionary are listed in **alphabetical order.**
- **Guide words** appear at the top of each dictionary page. Guide words show the first and last entry on the page.
   EXAMPLE: The word <u>dog</u> would appear on a dictionary page with the guide words <u>dodge</u> / <u>doll</u>. The word <u>dull</u> would not.

A. Put a check in front of each word that would be listed on the dictionary page with the given guide words.

1. frozen / gather

_____ fruit
_____ grain
_____ furnish
_____ gate
_____ gallon
_____ former
_____ forgive
_____ fuzz
_____ galaxy
_____ future

2. money / muscle

_____ muddy
_____ moss
_____ motorcycle
_____ mustard
_____ moisten
_____ moose
_____ museum
_____ morning
_____ mortal
_____ modest

3. perfect / pin

_____ perfume
_____ pit
_____ pick
_____ photo
_____ pest
_____ plastic
_____ pillow
_____ pile
_____ pipe
_____ pizza

B. Number the words in each column in the order in which they would appear in a dictionary. Then write the words that could be the guide words for each column.

1. _____ / _____

_____ raccoon
_____ radar
_____ rabbit
_____ raisin
_____ react
_____ reflect
_____ rebel
_____ rainfall
_____ relay
_____ remind
_____ refuse
_____ ran

2. _____ / _____

_____ seize
_____ shellfish
_____ shrink
_____ signal
_____ silent
_____ scent
_____ shuffle
_____ shaft
_____ serpent
_____ seldom
_____ scope
_____ selfish

3. _____ / _____

_____ octopus
_____ olive
_____ of
_____ office
_____ old
_____ odor
_____ once
_____ oil
_____ odd
_____ onion
_____ occasion
_____ only

Dictionary: Syllables

- A **syllable** is a part of a word that is pronounced at one time. Dictionary entry words are divided into syllables to show how they can be divided at the end of a writing line.
- A **hyphen (-)** is placed between syllables to separate them.
  EXAMPLE: man-a-ger
- If a word has a beginning or ending syllable of only one letter, do not divide it so that one letter stands alone.
  EXAMPLES: a-lone   sand-y

A. Write each word as a whole word.

1. ad-ver-tise _____

2. blun-der _____

3. par-a-dise _____

4. mis-chie-vous _____

5. con-crete _____

6. mi-cro-phone _____

7. in-ci-dent _____

8. val-ue _____

B. Find each word in a dictionary. Rewrite the word, placing a hyphen between each syllable.

1. bicycle _____

2. solution _____

3. category _____

4. punishment _____

5. behavior _____

6. quarterback _____

7. disappear _____

8. theory _____

9. wonderful _____

10. biology _____

11. sizzle _____

12. foreign _____

13. transparent _____

14. civilization _____

C. Write two ways in which each word may be divided at the end of a writing line.

1. mosquito   mos-quito   mosqui-to

2. ambition _____ _____

3. boundary _____ _____

4. gingerbread _____ _____

5. geography _____ _____

6. leadership _____ _____

Dictionary: Definitions and Parts of Speech

- A dictionary lists the **definitions** of each entry word. Many words have more than one definition. In this case, the most commonly used definition is given first. Sometimes a definition is followed by a sentence showing a use of the entry word.
- A dictionary also gives the **part of speech** for each entry word. An abbreviation (shown below) stands for each part of speech. Some words might be used as more than one part of speech.
  EXAMPLE: **frost** (frôst) *n.* **1.** frozen moisture. *There was frost on all the leaves.* *-v.* **2.** to cover with frosting. *I'll frost the cake when it's cool.*

- **Use the dictionary samples below to answer the questions.**

spec-i-fy (spes′ ə fī′) *v.* **1.** to say or tell in an exact way: *Please specify where we should meet you.* **2.** to designate as a specification: *The artist specified brown for the frame.*
spec-i-men (spes′ ə mən) *n.* **1.** a single person or thing that represents the group to which it belongs; example. **2.** a sample of something taken for medical purposes.

speck-le (spek′ əl) *n.* a small speck or mark. *-v.* to mark with speckles.
spec-tac-u-lar (spek tak′ yə lər) *adj.* relating to, or like a spectacle. *-n.* an elaborate show. —spec tac′ u lar ly, *adv.*

1. Which word can be used as either a noun or a verb? _____

2. Which word can be used only as a verb?

   _____

3. Which word can be used only as a noun?

   _____

n.	noun
pron.	pronoun
v.	verb
adj.	adjective
adv.	adverb
prep.	preposition

4. Which word can be used either as a noun or as an adjective? _____

5. Write a sentence using the first definition of spectacular. _____

   _____

6. Write a sentence using the first definition of specify. _____

   _____

7. Write a sentence using speckle as a verb. _____

   _____

8. Use the second definition of specimen in a sentence. _____

   _____

9. Which word shows an adverb form? _____

10. Which word shows two definitions used as a noun? _____

Dictionary: Word Origins

> ■ An **etymology** is the origin and development of a word. Many dictionary
> entries include etymologies. The etymology is usually enclosed in
> brackets [ ].
>> EXAMPLE: **knit** [ME *knitten* < OE *cnyttan,* to knot]. The word *knit*
>> comes from the Middle English word *knitten,* which came from the
>> Old English word *cnyttan,* meaning "to tie in a knot."

■ **Use these dictionary entries to answer the questions.**

cam-pus (kam′ pəs) *n.* the grounds and buildings of a school
or university. [Latin *campus,* meaning field, perhaps
because most colleges used to be in the country.]

chaise longue (shāz lông′) *n.* a chair with a long seat which
supports the sitter's outstretched legs. [French *chaise,* chair
+ *longue,* long.]

gar-de-nia (gär dēn′ yə) *n.* a fragrant yellow or white flower
from an evergreen shrub or tree. [Modern Latin *Gardenia,*
from Alexander *Garden,* 1730–1791, U.S. scientist who
studied plants.]

pas-teur-ize (pas′ chə rīz) *v.* to heat food to a high
temperature in order to destroy harmful bacteria. [From
Louis *Pasteur,* inventor of the process.]

rent (rent) *n.* a regular payment for the use of property.
[Old French *rente,* meaning taxes.]

ut-ter (ut′ ər) *v.* to express; make known; put forth. [From
Middle English or Dutch, *utteren,* literally, out.]

wam-pum (wom′ pəm) *n.* small beads made from shells
and used for money or jewelry. [Short for Algonquin
wampompeag, meaning strings of money.]

1. Which word comes from an Algonquin word? _____

2. What does the Algonquin word mean? _____

3. Which word was formed from the name of an inventor? _____

4. Which word comes from French words? _____

5. What do the French words <u>chaise</u> and <u>longue</u> mean? _____

6. Which word was formed from the name of a scientist? _____

7. Which word is short for the word <u>wampompeag</u>? _____

8. Which words come from Latin words? _____

9. Which word comes from a Middle English word? _____

10. What does the French word <u>rente</u> mean? _____

11. Which word comes from two languages? _____

12. What does the word <u>utteren</u> mean? _____

13. What does the Latin word <u>campus</u> mean? _____

14. Which word is the name of a flower? _____

15. Which word names a piece of furniture? _____

Name _____   Date _____

Using Parts of a Book

> - A **title page** lists the name of a book and its author.
> - A **copyright page** tells who published the book, where it was published, and when it was published.
> - A **table of contents** lists the chapter or unit titles and the page numbers on which they begin. It is at the front of a book.
> - An **index** gives a detailed list of the topics in a book and the page numbers on which each topic is found. It is in the back of a book.

A. Answer the questions below.

1. Where would you look to find when a book was published? _____

2. Where would you look to find the page number of a particular topic? _____

3. Where would you look to find the author's name? _____

4. Where would you look to find the titles of the chapters in a book? _____

B. Use the table of contents below to answer the questions.

Table of Contents

All Kinds of Plants 5	Grasses 24
Parts of Plants.....................7	Grains....................................26
Flowers 9	Medicines from Plants............30
Trees...................................15	Poisonous Plants...................32
Fruits 17	Protecting Plants 34
Vegetables.........................21	

1. What is this book about? _____

2. On what pages can you read about vegetables? _____

3. On what pages can you read about the parts of a plant? _____

4. On what pages can you read about trees? _____

5. What can you read about on page 24? _____

6. What can you read about on page 30? _____

7. On what pages can you read about poisonous plants? _____

8. On what page can you read about protecting plants? _____

9. What can you read about on page 17? _____

Name _____ Date _____

Using the Library

- Books on library shelves are arranged by **call numbers.** Each book is assigned a number from 000 to 999, according to its subject matter.
- The main subject groups for call numbers are as follows:

  000–099 Reference   500–599 Science and Math
  100–199 Philosophy   600–699 Technology
  200–299 Religion   700–799 The Arts
  300–399 Social Sciences   800–899 Literature
  400–499 Languages   900–999 History and Geography

A. Write the call number group in which you would find each book.

1. *A Guide to Electronics in a New Age*   _____

2. *A Traveler's Handbook of Everyday German*   _____

3. *World Almanac and Book of Facts*   _____

4. *A History of the Roman Empire*   _____

5. *The Modern Philosophers*   _____

6. *Religions of the World*   _____

7. *Solving Word Problems in Mathematics*   _____

8. *Folktales of Norway*   _____

9. *Painting with Watercolors*   _____

10. *People in Society*   _____

11. *Learn Spanish in Seven Days*   _____

12. *Science Experiments for the Beginner*   _____

13. *Technology in a New Century*   _____

14. *Funny Poems for a Rainy Day*   _____

15. *The Continent of Africa*   _____

B. Write the titles of three of your favorite books. Write the call number group beside each title.

1. _____

2. _____

3. _____

Using the Card Catalog

- The **card catalog** contains information cards on every book in the library. Some libraries are now computerized and have no card catalogs. But the information in the computer is filed in the same manner as the information in the card catalog.
- Each book has three cards in the catalog. They are filed separately according to:
  1. the author's last name
  2. the subject of the book
  3. the title of the book

A. Use the sample catalog card to answer the questions.

Author Card

Call number ——— 920.067   Hoobler, Dorothy and Thomas ——— Author
Title ——— Images across the ages: African portraits; illustrated by
John Gampert. – Austin : Raintree/Steck-Vaughn ——— Publisher
Date published ——— © 1993 ——— Place published
Number of pages ——— 96 p. : illus. ——— Illustrated

1. What are the authors' names? _____

2. What is the title of the book? _____

3. How many pages does the book have? _____

4. What is the call number of the book? _____

5. When was the book published? _____

6. What subject might this book be filed under? _____

B. Write author, title, or subject to tell which card you would look for to locate the book or books.

1. books about national parks in the United States _____

2. *The Adventures of Huckleberry Finn* _____

3. a novel by Sylvia Cassidy _____

4. books about Helen Keller _____

5. a book of poems by Vachel Lindsay _____

6. *Children's Verse in America* _____

Using an Encyclopedia

> ■ An **encyclopedia** is a reference book that contains articles on many different subjects. The articles are arranged alphabetically in volumes. Each volume is marked to show which articles are inside.
> ■ Guide words are used to show the first topic on each page.
> ■ At the end of most articles there is a listing of cross-references to related topics for the reader to investigate.

■ **Read each sample encyclopedia entry below. Then refer to each to answer the questions that follow.**

> **BIRDSEYE,** Clarence (1886–1956), was an American food expert and inventor. Birdseye was born in Brooklyn, N.Y., and educated at Amherst College. He is best known for developing methods of preserving foods and for marketing quick-frozen foods. He also worked on lighting technology, wood-pulping methods, and heating processes. *See also* FOOD PROCESSING.

1. Whom is the article about? _____

2. When did he live? _____

3. Where did he go to college? _____

4. What is he best known for? _____

5. What else did he work on? _____

6. What other article in the encyclopedia is related to the subject? _____

> **FOOD PROCESSING** is a process by which food is protected from spoiling for future use. Preserved food should look, taste, and feel like the original food. Many methods are used today to preserve food.
> **Canning** In this process, food is sterilized through heat treatments and sealed in airtight containers. Canned food stored in the cold of Antarctica was preserved for 50 years. This would not be true of canned food stored in hot climates.
> **Freezing** The freezing process was not widely used until the late 19th century. Freezing does not kill all types of bacteria, and care must be taken that foods are not thawed and refrozen. Freezing has the advantage of keeping food looking more like the fresh product than canning does.

7. Why do you think this cross-reference is included in the article about Birdseye?

_____

_____

8. Does the above cross-reference mention Clarence Birdseye? _____

Name _____   Date _____

Finding an Encyclopedia Article

When looking for an article in the encyclopedia:
- Always look up the last name of a person.
  EXAMPLE: To find an article on Helen Keller, look under Keller.
- Look up the first word in the name of a city, state, or country.
  EXAMPLE: To find an article on Puerto Rico, look under Puerto.
- Look up the most specific word in the name of a geographical location.
  EXAMPLE: To find an article on Lake Erie, look under Erie.
- Look up the most significant word in the name of a general topic.
  EXAMPLE: To find an article on neon lamps, look under neon.

A. The example below shows how the volumes of a particular encyclopedia are marked to indicate the alphabetical range of the articles they cover. Write the number of the volume in which you would find each article.

A	B	C–CH	CI–CZ	D	E	F	G	H	I–J	K	L
1	2	3	4	5	6	7	8	9	10	11	12

M	N	O	P	Q–R	S–SH	SI–SZ	T	U–V	W–X–Y–Z
13	14	15	16	17	18	19	20	21	22

1. camping _____   6. John F. Kennedy _____   11. Caspian Sea _____

2. North Dakota _____   7. Mount Kilimanjaro _____   12. Smith College _____

3. Jonathan Swift _____   8. sand flea _____   13. Victor Hugo _____

4. giant panda _____   9. New Guinea _____   14. elementary school _____

5. Nova Scotia _____   10. Babe Ruth _____   15. Lake Ontario _____

B. Look up the following articles in an encyclopedia. Write a cross-reference for each article.

1. bee _____   5. Georgia _____

2. X-ray _____   6. space travel _____

3. atom _____   7. Susan B. Anthony _____

4. music _____   8. cartoon _____

C. Choose a person who interests you, and find the entry for that person in an encyclopedia. Then answer the questions below.

1. Who is the person you've chosen? _____

2. When did this person live? _____

3. What made this person famous? _____

4. What encyclopedia did you use? _____

Name _____   Date _____

Using a Thesaurus

> ■ A **thesaurus** is a reference book that writers use to find the exact words they need. Like a dictionary, a thesaurus lists its entry words alphabetically. Each entry word has a list of **synonyms,** or words that can be used in its place. Some thesauruses also list **antonyms** for the entry word.
> EXAMPLE: You have just written the following sentence: The spectators **looked** from the sidelines.
> With the help of a thesaurus, you could improve the sentence by replacing looked with its more precise synonym watched.
> The spectators **watched** from the sidelines.

A. Use the thesaurus sample below to answer the questions.

> **heat** *n. syn.* warmth, fire, flame, fever, emotion, glow, blush, redness. *ant.* cold, coolness, ice, chilliness

1. Which is the entry word? _____

2. What are its synonyms?_____

   _____

3. Which word would you use in place of blaze? _____

4. Which word would you use in place of temperature? _____

5. What are the antonyms of heat? _____

6. Which antonyms would you use in place of hotness? _____

7. What antonym would you use in place of hot? _____

B. Write synonyms of heat to complete the sentences.

1. Eleanor sat by the _____ in the fireplace.

2. Its _____ spread through her body as she relaxed.

3. She felt a warm _____ inside her.

4. Her skin began to show some _____ as she sat there longer.

5. She felt as if she had a _____ .

6. She moved farther away from the flickering _____ .

7. She looked in the mirror and saw the _____ on her face.

8. Happiness was the _____ she felt.

Choosing Reference Sources

- Use a **dictionary** to find the definitions and pronunciations of words, suggestions for word usage, and etymologies.
- Use an **encyclopedia** to find articles about many different people, places, and other subjects. Also use an encyclopedia to find references to related topics.
- Use an **atlas** to find maps and other information about geographical locations.

■ Write encyclopedia, dictionary, or atlas to show which source you would use to find the following information. Some topics might be found in more than one source.

1. the pronunciation of the word measure _____

2. the location of Yellowstone National Park _____

3. the care and feeding of a dog _____

4. the distance between Rome and Naples _____

5. jewelry throughout the ages _____

6. planning a vegetable garden _____

7. the meaning of the word federal _____

8. the etymology of the word consider _____

9. the early life of Abraham Lincoln _____

10. the states through which the Mississippi River flows _____

11. how volcanoes form _____

12. a definition of the word ape _____

13. the rivers and mountains of Canada _____

14. how paper is made _____

15. the location of the border between Vermont and New Hampshire _____

16. the history of kite making _____

17. the pronunciation of the word particular _____

18. the names of lakes in Northern California _____

19. the meanings of the homographs of bow _____

20. methods of scoring in football _____

Name _____ Date _____

Unit 6 Test

Refer to the dictionary samples to answer the questions that follow.

leav-en (lev′en) *n.* **1.** a substance that causes dough to rise. **2.** a small piece of such dough put aside to be used for causing other dough to rise. *-v.* to cause dough to rise. [Middle English, from Old French, from Latin *levein.*]
left (left) *adj.* toward the side of the body that is westward when

facing north. *-n.* that which is on the left. *-adv.* toward the left. [Middle English *lift*, from Old English *lyft*, weak.]
let (let) *v.* **1.** to permit or allow: *Did he let you go?* **2.** to allow to pass through: *I let the bird out of its cage.* **3.** to make; cause: *They'll let us know.* **4.** to rent. [Old English *laeten*, to allow.]

1. Which word has two syllables?

   A ○ leaven   B ○ left   C ○ let

2. Which pair of words could be guide words for the entries above?

   A ○ length/liar   B ○ lay/lean   C ○ leaf/level

3. Which word has the most definitions?

   A ○ leaven   B ○ let   C ○ left

4. As which part of speech can left not be used?

   A ○ pronoun   B ○ adjective   C ○ adverb

5. Which word originally meant "weak"?

   A ○ let   B ○ left   C ○ leaven

6. From how many other languages did leaven come?

   A ○ two   B ○ three   C ○ four

Choose the correct answer to each question.

7. Where would you find the publisher of a book?   A ○ title page   B ○ index   C ○ copyright page

8. Where would you find chapter titles?   A ○ table of contents   B ○ index   C ○ title page

Tell which kind of catalog card you would refer to in order to find the book(s). Choose (A) for author card, (B) for subject card, or (C) for title card.

9. books about volcanoes in Hawaii   A ○   B ○   C ○

10. *To Kill a Mockingbird*   A ○   B ○   C ○

11. a book of short stories by O. Henry   A ○   B ○   C ○

12. books about Grandma Moses   A ○   B ○   C ○

13. a book of poems by Carl Sandburg   A ○   B ○   C ○

14. *The Story of Martin Luther King*   A ○   B ○   C ○

Tell which reference you would use to find the following information. Choose (A) for dictionary, (B) for encyclopedia, (C) for atlas, or (D) for thesaurus.

15. the distance from Kansas City to Chicago   A ○   B ○   C ○   D ○

16. information about mural painting   A ○   B ○   C ○   D ○

17. the etymology of the word define   A ○   B ○   C ○   D ○

18. the history of doll collecting   A ○   B ○   C ○   D ○

19. an antonym for the word increase   A ○   B ○   C ○   D ○

20. the definition of the word technology   A ○   B ○   C ○   D ○

Use the sample catalog card to answer the questions.

```
┌─────────────────────────────────────────────────────┐
│            RAIN FOREST                                │
│  574.5                                                │
│  M235    Macdonald, Fiona                             │
│              New view: Rain forest–                   │
│          Austin, TX: Raintree/Steck-Vaughn, ©1994     │
│              32p.: col. illus.                        │
└─────────────────────────────────────────────────────┘
```

21. What kind of catalog card is this?

  A ○ author card   **C** ○ subject card
  B ○ title card   **D** ○ contents card

22. What is the author's last name?

  A ○ Fiona   **C** ○ Steck-Vaughn
  B ○ Macdonald   **D** ○ Forest

23. What is the call number?

  A ○ 574.5/M235   **C** ○ 32
  B ○ 1994   **D** ○ Austin, TX

24. Who is the publisher?

  A ○ Macdonald   **C** ○ Raintree/Steck-Vaughn
  B ○ Austin, TX   **D** ○ New View

Choose a volume in an encyclopedia where each article would be found.

A	B	C–CH	CI–CZ	D	E	F	G	H	I–J	K	L
1	2	3	4	5	6	7	8	9	10	11	12

M	N	O	P	Q–R	S–SH	SI–SZ	T	U–V	W–X–Y–Z
13	14	15	16	17	18	19	20	21	22

25. North Carolina

  A ○ 3   **C** ○ 13
  B ○ 4   **D** ○ 14

26. Mahatma Gandhi

  A ○ 8   **C** ○ 13
  B ○ 9   **D** ○ 14

27. Olympic Games

  A ○ 8   **C** ○ 18
  B ○ 15   **D** ○ 19

28. country music

  A ○ 3   **C** ○ 13
  B ○ 4   **D** ○ 22

Refer to the thesaurus sample to answer the questions.

```
┌─────────────────────────────────────────────────────┐
│  sweet adj. syn. pleasant, pure, fresh, sugary. ant.  │
│  sour, acid, unripe, harsh                            │
└─────────────────────────────────────────────────────┘
```

29. What is the entry word?

  A ○ pleasant   **C** ○ unripe
  B ○ sour   **D** ○ sweet

30. What is a synonym of the entry word?

  A ○ sour   **C** ○ sugary
  B ○ sweet   **D** ○ harsh

31. Which word would you use in place of charming?

  A ○ sour   **C** ○ pure
  B ○ pleasant   **D** ○ acid

32. Which word would you use in place of rough?

  A ○ harsh   **C** ○ fresh
  B ○ unripe   **D** ○ sweet

Answer Key

Assessment Test (Pages 8–11)
A. 1. A **2.** H **3.** S **4.** H **B.** can **C. 1.** S **2.** C **3.** P **4.** P **D. 1.** can not
2. they will **E.** curious **F.** b **G.** The words in bold should be circled.
1. IN, **Who**, is going **2.** E, **I**, feel **3.** IM, **(You)**, do worry **4.** D, **It**, is
H. 1. CP **2.** CS **I. 1.** RO **2.** I **3.** CS **J.** Underline: officer, person.
Circle: Paul, Judge Hawkins. **K.** friend's **L.** The words in bold should
be circled. **Nolan Ryan,** a baseball star **M.** The word in bold should
be circled. He **will** soon discover the error in his plan. **N. 1.** past
2. future **3.** present **O. 1.** flew, went **2.** drank, threw **3.** froze, broke
P. The words in bold should be circled. **1.** SP, **You 2.** IP, **Nobody**
3. PP, **her 4.** OP, **us Q. 1.** adjective **2.** adverb **3.** adverb **4.** adjective
R. 1. Can **2.** learn **3.** set **4.** laid **5.** doesn't **S.** The words in bold
should be circled. You can either wait **in** the car or **outside** the door.
T.
          832 Southern Star
          Helena, MT 95097
          Aug. 27, 19__

Dear Edward,
  I have the information you wanted. Did you ever think I'd get it to
you this quickly? Well, it's time I surprised you. Here's what you
should bring: six cartons of orange juice, forty-five paper cups, and
three bags of ice. What a breakfast party this will be!
          Your friend,
          Bill
U. Answers will vary. **V. 1.** 5 **2.** 1 **3.** 6 **4.** 2 **5.** 3 **6.** 4 **W.** title
X. 1. noun **2.** after **3.** care/carrot **4.** 2 **5.** car-pet
Y. 1. Carol Rawlins **2.** 979.132 R39 **3.** 1995 **4.** Raintree/
Steck–Vaughn **5.** 64 **Z. 1.** atlas or encyclopedia **2.** encyclopedia
3. dictionary **4.** card catalog **5.** dictionary **6.** card catalog or
encyclopedia

Unit 1: Vocabulary
Synonyms and Antonyms (P. 13)
A. Synonyms will vary. **B. 1.** begin **2.** fall **3.** sick **4.** tired **5.** close
C. Antonyms will vary. **D. 1.** heavy **2.** late **3.** kind **4.** empty
5. found
Homonyms (P. 14)
A. 1. beach **2.** deer **3.** weigh **4.** pane **5.** to, to, two **6.** knew, new
7. their **8.** ate, eight **9.** sea **10.** Ring **11.** here **12.** write, right
13. read **14.** buy, by **15.** tale **B. 1.** haul **2.** through **3.** week
4. they're or their **5.** herd **6.** hear **7.** buy or bye **8.** pain **9.** heel or
he'll **10.** blue **11.** flour **12.** stare **13.** pail **14.** wring **15.** sore
16. sail **17.** one **18.** I'll or isle **19.** road or rowed **20.** meat or mete
21. hour **22.** see **23.** write or rite **24.** piece **25.** know **26.** great
27. weigh or whey **28.** sent or scent **29.** do or due **30.** fourth
Homographs (P. 15)
A. 1. checks **2.** interest **3.** vault **4.** interest **5.** vault **6.** checks
B. Sentences will vary. **1.** a **2.** a **3.** a **4.** a **5.** b
Prefixes (P. 16)
A. Definitions will vary. **1.** impractical **2.** misbehave **3.** uneasy
4. nonviolent **5.** unusual **B.** Meanings will vary. **1.** un **2.** dis **3.** dis
4. mis **5.** pre **6.** re **7.** mis **8.** im **9.** non **10.** un **11.** in **12.** pre
Suffixes (P. 17)
A. Definitions will vary. **1.** mountainous **2.** helpful **3.** snowy
4. national **5.** knowledgeable **B.** Meanings will vary. **1.** able
2. less **3.** ous **4.** able **5.** ous **6.** able **7.** ous **8.** ful **9.** y **10.** less
11. al **12.** al
Contractions (P. 18)
A. 1. they're, they are **2.** won't, will not **3.** There's, There is
4. That's, That is; shouldn't, should not **5.** weren't, were not
6. doesn't, does not **7.** can't, cannot; it's, it is **8.** they've, they have;
they'll, they will **9.** It's, It is; aren't, are not **10.** they'd, they would

B. 1. I have, I've; I would, I'd **2.** It is, It's; what is, what's **3.** I will, I'll
4. does not, doesn't
Compound Words (P. 19)
A. Answers will vary. **B. 1.** forehead **2.** haircut **3.** everywhere
4. newsstand **5.** loudspeaker **6.** everything
Connotation/Denotation (P. 20)
A. 1. wonderful **2.** Brave **3.** fascinating **4.** hilarious **5.** smile
B. 1. cheap **2.** soggy **3.** nagged **4.** silly **5.** smirk **6.** frightened
C. 1. antique **2.** slender **3.** thrifty **4.** parade **5.** disaster **6.** sip
7. starving **8.** filthy
Idioms (P. 21)
A. 1. j **2.** i **3.** h **4.** a **5.** e **6.** f **7.** d **8.** g **9.** b **10.** c
B. Meanings will vary. **1.** in hot water **2.** beside themselves **3.** fly
off the handle **4.** shaken up **5.** talk turkey
Unit 1 TEST (Pages 22–23)
1. D **2.** A **3.** B **4.** C **5.** B **6.** C **7.** D **8.** A **9.** C **10.** B **11.** C **12.** B
13. D **14.** A **15.** C **16.** B **17.** D **18.** B **19.** C **20.** A **21.** A **22.** D **23.** B
24. C **25.** C **26.** B **27.** B **28.** D **29.** B **30.** A **31.** C **32.** B **33.** A **34.** C
35. B **36.** B

Unit 2: Sentences
Recognizing Sentences (P. 24)
S should precede the following sentences, and students should end
each with a period: 2, 5, 7, 9, 10, 11, 12, 13, 16, 19, 20, 21, 22, 24,
28, 29.
Types of Sentences (P. 25)
1. IN **2.** IN **3.** D **4.** D **5.** D **6.** IN **7.** D **8.** D **9.** IN **10.** IN **11.** D
12. D **13.** IN **14.** D **15.** IN **16.** D **17.** D **18.** IN **19.** D **20.** IN **21.** IN
22. D **23.** D **24.** IN **25.** D **26.** IN **27.** IN **28.** D
More Types of Sentences (P. 26)
1. IM **2.** IM **3.** E **4.** IM **5.** E **6.** IM or E **7.** IM **8.** IM **9.** IM **10.** IM
11. E **12.** IM **13.** E **14.** E **15.** E **16.** E **17.** E **18.** IM **19.** IM **20.** E
21. E **22.** IM **23.** E **24.** IM **25.** IM **26.** IM **27.** E **28.** E
Complete Subjects and Predicates (P. 27)
1. Bees / fly. **2.** Trains / whistle. **3.** artist / drew **4.** wind / blew
5. grandmother / made **6.** We / surely **7.** cookies / are **8.** letter /
came **9.** They / rent **10.** Jennifer / is **11.** team / won **12.** band /
played **13.** sky / is **14.** auctioneer / was **15.** lightning / startled
16. wind / howled **17.** dog / followed **18.** apartment / is **19.** We /
have **20.** team / deserves **21.** rangers / fought **22.** friend / taught
23. stars / make **24.** airplane / was **25.** children / waded
26. Park / is **27.** weather / is **28.** trees / were
Simple Subjects and Predicates (P. 28)
1. clap of thunder / frightened **2.** snow / covered **3.** We / drove
4. students / are making **5.** class / read **6.** women / were talking
7. album / has **8.** We / are furnishing **9.** trees on that lawn / are
10. Americans / are working **11.** manager / read **12.** Bill / brought
13. We / opened **14.** mechanics / worked **15.** butterflies / fluttered
16. child / spoke **17.** We / found **18.** part of the program / is
19. person / is working **20.** Sheryl / swam **21.** program / will begin
22. handle of this basket / is **23.** clock in the tower / strikes
24. farmhouse on that road / belongs **25.** game of the season / will
be played
Subjects and Predicates in Inverted Order (P. 29)
A. Sentences 1, 3, 4, 5, 6, 8, 9, 11, and 12 are in inverted order.
1. falls / the **2.** tree / are **3.** rolled / the **4.** marched / the **5.** are /
many **6.** ran / the **7.** He / hit **8.** hiked / the **9.** is / the **10.** fish /
jumped **11.** came / the **12.** came / the **B. 1.** The mist falls lightly.
2. The rocks rolled over and over. **3.** The band marched down the
street. **4.** Many birds are near the ocean. **5.** The kitten ran right
under the chair. **6.** The campers hiked along the ridge. **7.** The
stream is underground. **8.** The trucks came over the hill. **9.** The
rainbow came out.

Using Compound Subjects (P. 30)

A. Sentences 1, 2, 3, 4, 6, 7, 8, and 9 have compound subjects.
1. English settlers and Spanish settlers / came **2.** Trees and bushes / were **3.** The fierce winds and the cold temperatures / made **4.** The settlers and Native Americans / became **5.** Native Americans / helped **6.** Potatoes and corn / were **7.** English settlers and Spanish settlers / had **8.** Peanuts and sunflower seeds / are **9.** Lima beans and corn / are **10.** Zucchini / is **11.** Native Americans / also
B. 1. Gold and silver from the New World were sent to Spain.
2. France and the Netherlands staked claims in the Americas in the 1500s and 1600s. **3.** John Cabot and Henry Hudson explored areas of the Americas. **C.** Sentences will vary.

Using Compound Predicates (P. 31)

A. Sentences 2, 3, 4, 6, 8, 9, 11, and 12 have compound predicates.
1. students / organized **2.** They / discussed **3.** They / wrote **4.** invitations / were **5.** families / responded **6.** students / bought **7.** families / bought **8.** students / packed **9.** families / brought **10.** Everyone / participated **11.** They / ran **12.** Everyone / packed
B. 1. Caroline heard and memorized the music. **2.** Keith picked up and loaded the newspapers into his car. **3.** Larry studied and wrote down the names of the states. **C.** Sentences will vary.

Simple and Compound Sentences (P. 32)

A. Sentences 1, 3, 5, and 6 are simple. Sentences 2 and 4 are compound. **1.** world / are **2.** earth / is, it / is **3.** world / are **4.** We / cannot, we / cannot **5.** drink / comes **6.** water / is **B. 1.** The Pacific Ocean is the largest ocean in the world, and it covers more area than all the earth's land put together. **2.** Bodies of salt water that are smaller than oceans are called seas, gulfs, or bays, and these bodies of water are often encircled by land. **3.** Seas, gulfs, and bays are joined to the oceans, and they vary in size and depth. **4.** The Mediterranean is one of the earth's largest seas, and it is almost entirely encircled by the southern part of Europe, the northern part of Africa, and the western part of Asia.

Correcting Run-on Sentences (P. 33)

Sentences may vary. **1.** In 1860, the Pony Express started in St. Joseph, Missouri. The route began where the railroads ended. **2.** People in the West wanted faster mail service. The mail took six weeks by boat. **3.** Mail sent by stagecoach took about 21 days. The Pony Express averaged ten days. **4.** The Pony Express used a relay system. Riders and horses were switched at 157 places along the way to Sacramento, California. **5.** Because teenagers weighed less than adults, most of the riders were teenagers. The horses could run faster carrying them. **6.** Riders had to cross raging rivers. The mountains were another barrier.

Expanding Sentences (P. 34)

A. and B. Sentences will vary.

Unit 2 TEST (Pages 35–36)

1. B **2.** A **3.** D **4.** C **5.** B **6.** A **7.** A **8.** C **9.** D **10.** B **11.** A **12.** B **13.** C **14.** D **15.** C **16.** A **17.** A **18.** C **19.** B **20.** D **21.** C **22.** A **23.** B **24.** C **25.** A **26.** B **27.** C **28.** A **29.** A **30.** C **31.** C **32.** A

Unit 3: Grammar and Usage

Nouns (P. 37)

A. Answers will vary. **B. 1.** Alaska; gold; silver; copper; oil **2.** Chocolate; beans; tree; tropics **3.** distance; Texas; distance; Chicago; New York **4.** men; women; horses; parade **5.** city; California; San Diego **6.** Alexander Graham Bell; inventor; telephone; Edinburgh, Scotland **7.** Jack, Diane, plane; London; Buckingham Palace **8.** animals; piranhas; alligators; anacondas; sloths; Amazon River Basin **9.** tarantula; type; spider **10.** Maya; people; Mexico; Central America

Common and Proper Nouns (Pages 38–39)

A. Answers will vary. **B.** Answers will vary. Suggested: **1.** state **2.** continent **3.** day **4.** river **5.** person **6.** lake **7.** holiday **8.** ocean **9.** province **10.** person **11.** planet **12.** president **13.** month **14.** mountains **15.** country **16.** book **17.** person **18.** city **19.** city

20. dog **C. 1.** timber; oak; furniture; bridges; ships **2.** painter; jeweler; farmer; engineer; inventor **3.** crops; sugar; tobacco; coffee; fruits **4.** groves; nuts; part **5.** rivers; beaches **6.** bridge; world **7.** foods; lamb; fish; olives; cheese **8.** road; tunnel; base; tree **9.** civilizations; gold; ornaments **10.** lakes **11.** tree; blossoms; fruits **12.** center **13.** trees; turpentine; tar; resin; timber; oils **14.** amount; coffee **15.** pelican; penguin; flamingo; birds **16.** trip; space; danger
D. 1. Brazil **2.** William Penn; Pennsylvania **3.** Elm Grove Library **4.** Commander Byrd; North Pole **5.** Dr. Jeanne Spurlock; Howard University College of Medicine **6.** Europe; Asia **7.** Colombia **8.** Kilimanjaro; Africa **9.** Navajo **10.** Leticia; Carlos; Sam; Ted **11.** Thomas Jefferson; United States **12.** Lake Michigan **13.** Quebec; North America **14.** Paul Revere **15.** India **16.** Sears Tower; Chicago

Singular and Plural Nouns (Pages 40–41)

A. 1. newspapers **2.** guesses **3.** towns **4.** valleys **5.** bodies **6.** stories **7.** bushes **8.** offices **9.** taxes **10.** toys **11.** bosses **12.** schools **13.** days **14.** copies **15.** authors **16.** porches **B. 1.** pennies **2.** dresses **3.** bridges **4.** brushes **5.** counties **6.** foxes **7.** books **8.** lunches **9.** countries **C. 1.** knives **2.** loaves **3.** halves **4.** mice **5.** feet **6.** geese **7.** hooves **8.** moose **9.** lives **10.** tomatoes **11.** teeth **12.** pianos **D. 1.** feet **2.** sheep **3.** chimneys **4.** cities **5.** leaves **6.** mosquitoes **7.** nickels **8.** friends **9.** desks **10.** benches

Possessive Nouns (Pages 42–43)

A. 1. girl's **2.** child's **3.** women's **4.** children's **5.** John's **6.** baby's **7.** boys' **8.** teacher's **9.** Dr. Ray's **10.** ladies' **11.** brother's **12.** soldier's **13.** men's **14.** aunt's **15.** Ms. Jones's **B. 1.** Jim's cap **2.** Kathy's wrench **3.** baby's smile **4.** friend's car **5.** Kim's new shoes **6.** dog's collar **7.** Frank's golf clubs **8.** runners' shoes **9.** parents' friends **10.** editor's opinion **11.** children's lunches **12.** Kyle's coat **13.** teacher's assignment **C. 1.** company's **2.** dog's **3.** women's **4.** Doug's **5.** David's **6.** cat's **7.** Kurt's **8.** Men's **9.** squirrel's **10.** brother's **11.** child's **12.** calf's **13.** baby's **14.** teachers' **15.** Alex's **16.** deer's **17.** Stacy's **18.** country's **19.** robins' **20.** person's **21.** sister's **22.** children's **23.** neighbors' **24.** class's **25.** boys' **26.** designer's **27.** horse's

Appositives (P. 44)

A. Students should circle the phrases in bold. **1. my father's older brother,** Henry **2. the Missouri Pacific,** train **3. the location of the main station,** Seattle **4. its main cargo,** Coal and lumber **5. our uncle,** Henry **6. his nephews,** us **7. his brother,** father **8. his sister-in-law,** mother **9. his wife,** Aunt Emma **10. Todd and Elizabeth,** cousins **B.** Sentences will vary.

Verbs (P. 45)

1. are **2.** wrote **3.** Check **4.** have **5.** is **6.** reached **7.** won **8.** trains **9.** has **10.** are **11.** remember **12.** bought **13.** is **14.** followed **15.** whistled **16.** watches **17.** scored **18.** won **19.** is **20.** lays **21.** set **22.** Answer **23.** explained **24.** worked **25.** has **26.** plays **27.** Brush **28.** whirled **29.** arrived **30.** is

Verb Phrases (P. 46)

1. were held **2.** invented **3.** was **4.** was **5.** built **6.** will arrive **7.** was **8.** has made **9.** covered **10.** have ridden **11.** is molding **12.** spent **13.** are posted **14.** has found **15.** is going **16.** have trimmed **17.** exports **18.** is reading **19.** helped **20.** was discovered **21.** was called **22.** are planning **23.** has howled **24.** have arrived **25.** have written **26.** can name **27.** received **28.** was printed **29.** are working **30.** was painted

Helping Verbs (P. 47)

A. Students should circle the words in bold. **1. have** begun **2. will** rake **3. must** sweep **4. will** pull **5. may** prepare **6. should** wash **7. would** make **8. is** working **9. has** sprayed **10. must** close **11. would** enjoy **12. might** finish **B.** Sentences will vary.

More Helping Verbs (P. 48)

A. Students should circle the words in bold. **1. will be** given **2. have been** studying **3. may be** forming **4. should be** reviewing **5. Are** joining **6. May** meet **7. should have** known **8. have** been **9. have been** looking **10. would have** met **11. has been** delayed